To Connie & Roger

Happy 25th

Love JoAnne & Raul

This was
PIONEER
MOTORING

"Few material things have been as important to America as the automobile. The manufacture of the automobile was the root of our industrial growth, and for decades now it has been the central support of our economy. We are all tied to the automobile by history, by business, by emotion. The automobile deserves to be preserved and remembered."

WILLIAM F. HARRAH
in Automotive Old Timers News

Shown above is the press car (Model 30 Packard) of the 1908 Glidden Tour stopped to permit begoggled occupants to enjoy roadside refreshments, long before era of drive-ins. (John A. Conde Collection) . . . In the pioneer days of motoring (opposite) only the daring ventured out in open-air vehicles during winter months. (American Motors Corp.)

This was
PIONEER
MOTORING

by

ROBERT F. KAROLEVITZ

An Album of Nostalgic Automemorabilia

SUPERIOR PUBLISHING COMPANY ● SEATTLE

Library of Congress Card Catalogue Number 68-22359

FIRST EDITION

Printed in the United States of America

DEDICATED

to my daughters

JAN *and* JILL

two Space Age youngsters who can't quite compre-
hend what life was like before television—but who
have kept their father interested in history with a
simple childish request:

"Tell us about the olden days, Daddy!"

Right-hand drive Stanley Steamer helped introduce new diversion—the scenic tour—to Americans everywhere. C. L. McClure snapped this historic photo (above) in Estes Park, Colo. (Denver Public Library Western Collection).

Before we start . . .

This, obviously, is neither the first nor the last book to be written on the subject of pioneer automobiles. The field is so broad . . . and the interest so intense . . . that the stories are virtually unending.

In this instance, we are not attempting to do an all-encompassing history of motorized transportation. Neither are we recording a step-by-step, detail-by-detail saga of a complex, gigantic industry which affects everyone in our society one way or another.

Instead, this is simply a book of nostalgia. To retread a cliche, it is an automotive trip down memory lane . . . a pictorial recalling of the way things were when the horse and his putt-putting competition were sharing the same city streets and country roadways.

The main purpose of the volume is to preserve between two covers some of the excellent old photographs which epitomize this wonderful era of transition when animal and mechanical power crossed paths in history, going in opposite directions. Words—no matter how well chosen—can little embellish a picture of a Brush Runabout mired wooden-axle deep in a muddy morass called a highway . . . or a team of horses hitched to a recalcitrant Rainier or Rickenbacker which failed to respond to a driver's frantic coaxings.

Generally, we have been less interested in technical specifications and picayunish detail than in the creation of a mood. Some writer has said that "looking back is done by those who have nothing to look forward to"—but we disagree! A little reminiscence is good for everyone, if for no other reason than to appreciate just how far we've come.

Depending upon your generation, we hope the ensuing pages will spur some personal memories . . . or provide graphic evidence of how your parents or grandparents traveled in the "good old days"—when a cloverleaf meant vegetable matter and not concrete, and when much of the nation's horsepower was still generated by four steel-shod hooves.

ROBERT F. KAROLEVITZ

A Word of Thanks

There are a few uninitiated individuals who think that books of this type "just sort of happen;" that somehow all the various pieces come together with a modicum of fretting and sweating.

Those of us who, in our weaker moments, agree to projects like this, only **wish** that were the case!

My wife, Phyllis, can tell you, for instance, that there are mountains of letters to write, loads of books to haul back and forth between home and library, stacks of manuscript sheets and cutlines to type, cartons of pictures to sort and re-sort and an ever-present coffee pot to tend. Once again she survived another production, kept household morale on a reasonably even keel and goaded a sometimes-laggard husband into editorial action. She knows I am grateful; she is—as I teasingly say—tops on my succor list.

There are others who have been most helpful to me: Ralph B. Sunde, inveterate auto hobbyist of Sioux Falls, South Dakota, who showed up at just the right time with his collection of old-car trade journals, collectors magazines and club journals; John A. Conde of the American Motors Corporation, who provided numerous pictures from company and personal archives; Don H. Berkebile of The Smithsonian Institution's Division of Transportation, who sent photos, information and encouragement.

Frank Perrin, public relations manager of the Great Northern Railway Company, ransacked the archives to find materials for the 1913 Glidden Tour story; and Eugene D. Becker, curator of pictures for the Minnesota Historical Society, generously researched his files above and beyond the call. Artist Emmet F. Billings gave up valuable fishing time to letter the automobile nameplates which appear on page 124.

There were dozens of others, of course, who responded to my requests for assistance. To all those listed below (and any I may have inadvertently overlooked), I say a hearty "thank you!"

Aiders and Abettors . . .

James P. Aehl, *J. I. Case Company*
Ernest L. Arms, *Sears, Roebuck and Company*
Martha L. Ayers, *THE BULB HORN, The Veteran Motor Car Club of America*
Fred R. Bell, *U.S. National Park Service*
F. W. Bennetts, *Oldsmobile Division, General Motors Corporation*
Rolf A. Blank, *Young & Rubicam, Inc. (for International Harvester)*
Edward J. Boucher, *Department of State Highways, Michigan.*
Mr. and Mrs. Jorgen Bruget, *Gayville, South Dakota*
Tad Burness, *San Jose, California*
Tom M. Campbell, *Cities Service Oil Company*
Mary M. Cattie, *The Free Library of Philadelphia*
Wilfrid M. Collins, *Cadillac Motor Car Division, General Motors Corporation*
Peter Craigmoe, *Union Oil Company of California*
Virginia Daiker, *The Library of Congress*
Arthur J. Danley, *FWD Corporation*
William B. deMeza, *The Goodyear Tire & Rubber Company*
Donald E. Dobbs, *The Prestolite Company*
William C. Dredge, *Studebaker Corporation*
William Dugovich, *Washington State Highway Commission*

R. W. Emerick, *Pontiac Motor Division, General Motors Corp.*
Robert L. Gamble, *Utility Trailer Manufacturing Company*
Chester Gibbon, *THE SEATTLE TIMES*
Mrs. Gail M. Gibson, *Pennsylvania Historical and Museum Commission*
Charles W. Granger, *Milwaukee, Wisconsin*
Betty L. Hale, *Mobil Oil Corporation*
Jack D. Haley, *University of Oklahoma Western History Collections*
Tobi Halpern, *National Safety Council*
Zenon C. R. Hansen, *President, Mack Trucks, Inc.*
M. M. Herrick, *Johnson Service Company*
John A. Kinley, *Eaton Yale & Towne, Inc.*
C. W. Lyman, *Portland Cement Association*
Chas. Lytle, *Sharon, Pennsylvania*
Bruce MacDonald, *Fisher Body Division, General Motors Corp.*
Colleen Majors, *North Dakota Historical Society*
James McCready, *The B. F. Goodrich Company*
K. E. McCullam, *Texaco, Inc.*
Theodore H. Mecke, Jr., *Ford Motor Company*

L. O. Merrill, *San Mateo County Historical Association*
Edward J. Mulligan, *American Petroleum Institute*
Henry L. Norton, *THE MILWAUKEE JOURNAL*
James W. Phillips, *Seattle, Wash.*
Bruce Quayle, *Sinclair Oil Corp.*
Robert W. Richmond, *Kansas State Historical Society*
F. H. Roberts, *Shell Oil Company*
Dorothy M. Ross, *Automotive Old Timers, Inc.*
Lynn Ruester, *Buick Motor Division, General Motors Corporation*
Irene Simpson, *Wells Fargo Bank History Room*
Norman E. Snyder, *Delco Products, General Motors Corporation*
Jean Sonnhalter, *The Firestone Tire & Rubber Company*
Sue Suib, *The Port of New York Authority*
Edwin J. Sunde, *Minneapolis, Minn.*
E. R. Tarnowsky, *Harrah's Automobile Collection*
Don Thielke, *Allis-Chalmers Manufacturing Company*
R. W. Tupper, *American Automobile Association*
Larry A. Viskochil, *Chicago Historical Society*
B. Jack Werre, *Standard Oil Company of California*
Leonard Westrate, *Chevrolet Motor Division, General Motors Corp.*
Martin L. Whitmyer, *Chrysler Corp.*

PARTS LIST

Dedication 5

Before We Start 7

A Word of Thanks 8

What on Earth Will We Call It? 11

Automoguls: Men Behind the Machines 23

Old Dobbin Gets a Final Horse Laugh 41

Survival—of the Fittest and Fleetest! 51

    Odyssey of Old Scout and Old Steady 65

    The Glidden Tours: One Last Grand Gasp ... 73

Ruts They Called Roads 81

Symbol of an Era: The Triumphant T 95

Tires Patched, Tanks Filled, Horses Shod 105

What's Your Hurry, Bud? 121

Wanderlust and Whoop-De-Do! 131

At Work and at War 143

The Smell of Perfume and Petrol 157

Chiefs and Indians on Wheels 167

The End of the Beginning 177

Slogans of Note 186

Bibliography 187

Index 188

Massive White Steamer, dainty electric (with Thomas A. Edison boarding) and gas-operated Cartercar epitomized three major power sources for early day autos (top and left bottom) . . . To be able to pose in real motor car (right bottom) at Alaska-Yukon-Pacific Exposition in Seattle in 1909 was thrill of a lifetime. (Photos, top left—American Automobile Assn.; top right, The Smithsonian Institution; bottom left, Edwin J. Sunde Collection; bottom right, Chester Gibbon Collection).

WOONSOCKET, SOUTH DAKOTA, did not emerge as an auto building center, but E. S. Callihan was said to have had this three-wheeled steamer on streets of that tiny prairie town as early as 1884. (Minnesota Historical Society).

WHAT ON EARTH
shall we call it?

Consider the plight of the earliest builders of self-propelled vehicles. When they made one, they didn't have a name for it!

Like all new discoveries, motorized transportation demanded a specialized vocabulary to make communication possible. In some respects, the language of the automobile had as much of a stuttering start as the pioneer contraptions themselves.

Imagine what would have happened had Oliver Evans of Philadelphia (who had applied for a U.S. patent on a "Steam Land Carriage" in 1792) achieved popular success back in 1805. That was the year he was commissioned by the city's board of health to build a versatile steam-driven river dredge. His added idea was that the machine would also travel on land under its own power. His concept included the mounting of a cumbersome flatboat onto a heavy seaworthy wagon; a series of belts and gears transmitted the power of the boat's engine to the wagon wheels. Evans called his 40,000-pound contrivance an **Oruktor Amphibolos!**

Had his ideas been practical, we could have had an entirely different idiom. Newspaper headlines might have proclaimed:

**ORUKTOR ACCIDENT
CLAIMS SIX LIVES**

**SURVEYS INDICATE UPSURGE
IN ORUKTORING IN THE U.S.**

**UNITED ORUKTOR WORKERS
STRIKE AT DETROIT PLANT**

Partly because of financing difficulties, the Evans vehicle never caught on; neither did his nomenclature. In 1813, though, he was prophetic enough to write: "The time will come when people will travel in stages moved by steam engines, from one city to another almost as fast as birds fly, 15 to 20 miles in an hour."

There were others like him—imaginative individuals in Europe and the United States—who could visualize the possibilities of road travel without the use of animal power. But they, too, were historically premature, as their philosophies and prototype machines were laughed at, frowned upon and legislated against. Among them was Nicholas Joseph Cugnot, who, with the blessings and finances of the French

FIRST OLDSMOBILE built by Olds Motor Vehicle Company was rolled out of tiny shop on River Street in Lansing, Mich., in 1897. It gave little indication of greater things to come when posed on tarp for the photographer. (Oldsmobile Division, General Motors Corporation).

government, built a steam-propelled, three-wheeled artillery wagon in 1769. It worked—but in a demonstration run it went out of control at less than three miles-per-hour, ran into a wall and, in the end, burdened the visionary inventor with more public relations and legal problems than the venture was worth. Still, the teakettle-on-wheels was a **beginning!** Most historians of self-driven land transportation trace the genesis of the automobile back to Cugnot and his unique cannon tractor.

In England there was Richard Trevithick, the Cornish mine official who tested his first steam car in a Christmas Eve snowfall at Camborne in 1801. He later built a second vehicle with drive wheels 10 feet in diameter. In New York City at mid-century Richard Dudgeon was experimenting with steam-mobiles, one of which was destroyed by fire in 1858 in the famed Crystal Palace, and the other—built almost a decade later—reputedly banned from the streets by civic officials.

It takes courage to effect revolutionary changes of any kind, and there were some indomitable tinkerers in the horse-dominated nineteenth century. Men like William Murdock, William Henry James, William Symington, Sir Goldsworthy Gurney and Walter Hancock in England; Charles Dallery, Etienne Lenoir and Amedee Bollee-Pere of France; Siegfried Marcus, a German Jew who lived most of his life in Austria; Thomas Blanchard, William Janes, Nathan Read, eccentric Apollos Kinsey and Silvester H. Roper in the United States; and, of course, Carl Benz and Gottlieb Daimler, the meticulous persevering Germans who were so instrumental in the adaptation of the internal combustion engine to horseless, trackless vehicles.

This, however, is not meant to be a detailed history of the germination and development of motorized transport. The story is so complex, so intertwined that it may never be completely unsnarled. There were so many men in various parts of the world laboring to accomplish the same general goal that the achievements and contributions of each have been difficult, if not impossible, to trace chronologically. That's why the emphasis is usually on such highlights as these:

1860—Etienne Lenoir built and patented in France the first commercially satisfactory gas engine. (Two years later he actually constructed a crude vehicle on which he tested his engine.)

1875—Siegfried Marcus of Austria built his second gasoline-powered vehicle which is still preserved in the Technical Museum in Vienna; the details and success of an earlier car in 1864 are debatable.

1876—In Deutz, Germany, Eugene Langen and Nikolaus August Otto introduced the four-stroke Otto silent engine; Gottlieb Daimler, an employee of Langen and Otto, was involved in the engine's design.

1879—George B. Selden, an attorney in Rochester, New York (who at that time had never built a motor vehicle), applied for and ultimately received U.S. Patent No. 549,160 (1895); as a result, claims against manufacturers of automobiles clouded the industrial scene for years.

1885—Carl Benz successfully tested his first gasoline engine auto at Mannheim, Germany.

1886—In Bad Cannstatt, Germany, Gottlieb Daimler built and operated a four-wheeled car propelled by a one-cylinder engine. (The previous year he and Wilhelm Maybach had successfully used a similar engine on a wooden bicycle.)

1893—Charles E. and J. Frank Duryea introduced what has generally been recognized as America's first successful internal combustion horseless carriage at Springfield, Massachusetts. (John William Lambert of Ohio City, Ohio—who held more than 600 patents relating to automobiles and other machinery—is said to have completed a three-wheeled gas-driven vehicle as early as 1891.)

1895—The Duryea brothers established the Duryea Motor Wagon Company, the first firm in America organized to make gas cars commercially.

1901—Ransom E. Olds became the first mass-producer of gasoline automobiles with the completion of 425 curved-dash Oldsmobiles in a single year.

1902—The American Automobile Association was organized in Chicago on March 4, symbolizing the broad interest in the new mode of transportation.

1908—The Model T Ford was unveiled for the first time on October 1.

There were dozens of other milestones, of course—many of them with a European locale. Great Britain's infamous "Red Flag Law" of 1865, for instance, was notable because of its stifling effect on the development of self-propelled road vehicles in the British Isles. This Locomotives on Highways Act (as it was officially known) limited the speed of mechanical vehicles to two miles-per-hour in towns and four miles-per-hour in the country. Of the three persons required to accompany each "road locomotive," one had to walk 60 yards ahead of the contrivance carrying a red flag by day and a red lantern at night. For four decades this restrictive legislation kept British inventors from competing with those on the Continent.

In America, automotive advancement was hampered by the lack of roads. Bicyclists, however, generated a national good roads movement in the early 1890s, culminating with the establishment of the U.S. Office of Road Inquiry under the Department of Agriculture in 1893. (This office later evolved into the Bureau of Public Roads.)

During this formative period, the word-smiths were having their problems, too. If machines-on-wheels were to become a common sight on city streets and country byways, they would certainly need a generic name.

George Selden's patent was for a "road machine." The Duryea brothers called their first products "motor wagons." In 1896 Henry Ford introduced an experimental car labeled the Quadricycle. **The Motocycle,** published in Chicago, was one of the first American automotive trade journals. Newspaper stories of the era used words like autometon, mocole, oleo locomotive, autokenetic, buggyaut, motor carriage, motor-vique, automotor horse, diamote, motorig, autobaine and, of course, horseless carriage.

In 1895 H. H. Kohlsaat, publisher of the **Chicago Times-Herald,** promoted the first horseless buggy race in America. As an added fillip, he offered $500 for the best all-encompassing name for the motorized vehicles of the day. The judges picked "motocycle" as the winner. "Quadricycle" was highly favored and "petrocar" earned a few votes. The French word, "automobile," wasn't even in the running!

In less than a year, however, it was the latter designation which began to appear more and more in public print in the United States. The **New York Times** prophesied in 1897:

> . . . the new mechanical wagon with the awful name—automobile . . . has come to stay . . . sooner or later they will displace the fashionable carriage of the present hour . . . Sensitive and emotional folk cannot view the impending change without conflicting emotions. Man loves the horse and he is not likely to love the automobile . . . nor will he ever get quite used, in this generation, to speeding along the road behind nothing.

More by linguistic phenomenon than promotional effort, "automobile" caught on. In its first edition in October, 1899, **The Automobile Magazine** editorialized:

For generic purposes the word "automobile" could hardly be improved upon. Objection is made that it is French. It is true that the name originated in France, where it has the official sanction of so scholarly and conservative a body as the French Academy, the supreme authority in French orthography. But while it is proper that the country where the automobile was born should give a universal name to its child, it happens that "automobile" is also good and intelligible English . . .

The same magazine defended the expression "automobilism" as an acceptable term to cover all phases of motoring. The editors, however, were not favorably disposed to "mobe" as a diminutive for "automobile." They likened it to "bike" for "bicycle" which they also denounced as harsh and "unlovely."

Life magazine in 1901 even used the word "automobility" to refer to the class of people caught up in the new craze.

But call it what they would, the automobile (as the **New York Times** predicted) was here to stay! No amount of semantic bickering could alter the relentless desire for motorization. The horse—so well thought of through the centuries—suddenly lost his popularity, and (for better or for worse) a new era in transportation dawned.

ONE-CYLINDER BRUSH, circa 1910, with wooden front axle and coil springs all around. (Pennsylvania Historical and Museum Commission).

Started February 16-1892 . Completed June 20-1892

DON H. BERKEBILE of The Smithsonian Institution's Division of Transportation discovered evidence that this Harris motor wagon, built in Baltimore in 1892, operated successfully before Duryea brothers' car. Sightseeing bus rather than conventional auto, Harris vehicle nonetheless must certainly be included in chronology of American automotive development. (The Smithsonian Institution).

CURVED-DASH OLDSMOBILE was America's first quantity-produced automobile. Ransom E. Olds (left) and J. D. Maxwell, after whom another famous pioneer auto was named, tested 1901 model for hill climbing ability. A little "body English" helped! (Photos Oldsmobile Div., General Motors Corp.)

VINTAGE LOCOMOBILE (above) somehow showed up in Dismal Swamp, Norfolk Co., Virginia. Probably staged, picture does illustrate rapid spread of motor car to remotest hinterlands. (Minnesota Historical Society) . . . Historians continue to discover pioneer builders among earliest to get their cars on road. While more publicized individuals like the Duryeas, Appersons and Ford were working on their embryonic designs, Stephen M. Balger (below left) was also introducing concept which was, in effect, two bicycles in parallel, powered by 3-cyl. gas engines. (The Smithsonian Institution) . . . First Baker Electric was manufactured by Baker Motor Vehicle Company of Cleveland, Ohio, just before turn of century. Electric car builders promoted simplicity of operation (below center), emphasizing that even a child could run one. (The Free Library of Philadelphia).

THE STUDEBAKER NAME was applied to vehicles as early as 1852 when the products were wagons, buggies and carriages. In 1899 firm entered auto industry as body-maker. 3 years later it produced its first car, an electric runabout. (Studebaker Corporation) . . . Alexander Winton, bicycle builder in Cleveland, Ohio, produced his first experimental car in 1896. Year later he formed The Winton Motor Carriage Company, started to market two-seaters like this dos-a-dos model (below). B. F. Goodrich made the pioneer pneumatic tires. (The B. F. Goodrich Company).

SEEMINGLY OVERNIGHT automobiles of every shape and description began to appear on city streets and country roads. Sidewalk gawkers—pedestrians of an earlier generation—always stopped to stare (above) when the strange contraptions went by. In few short years, however, autos became so commonplace they seldom rated second glance. (American Automoble Assn.) . . . Pioneer designers experimented with seating arrangements as they did with all other details of first cars. Not most practical was this two-seater (below left) shown on streets of Boulder, Colo. Lady passengers served as windbreakers but did not help driver's vision. (Denver Public Library Western Collection) . . . Home-made autos turned up in most unusual locales. This high-seater (below right) made its appearance in Moundridge, Kansas, circa 1898. (The Kansas State Historical Society).

HENRY FORD, farm boy mechanic turned auto magnate, created his first experimental gas car in this small Detroit workshop (above), now preserved for historical value. The Quadricycle (shown below with inventor at tiller) was completed in 1896, predecessor of millions of Fords. (Photos Ford Motor Company)

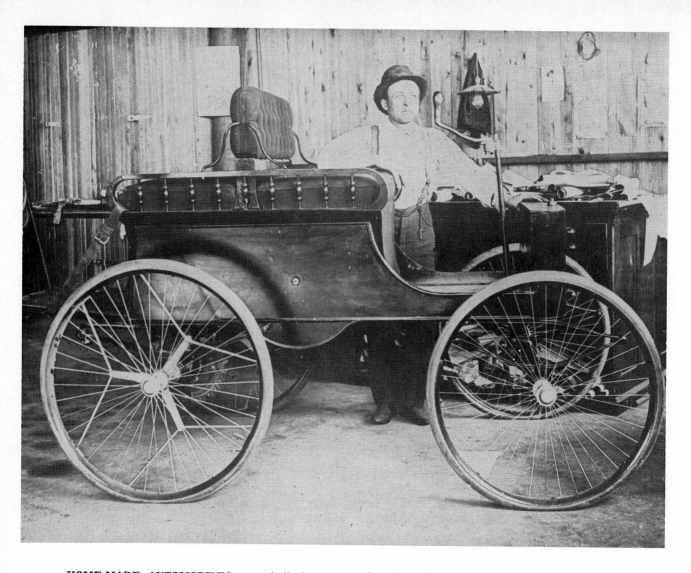

HOME-MADE AUTOMOBILES were built by unremembered mechanics and hopeful inventors everywhere. Many of them were one-timers that never made it to market. This nameless one (above) featured special rear wheel bracing. (Minnesota Historical Society) . . . Some historians argue that John W. Lambert's three-wheeled jitney should supersede Duryea car as America's first successful gas-mobile. Walter Lewis photographed controversial vehicle (below) in 1891 in Ohio City, Ohio. (The Smithsonian Institution).

THOMAS B. JEFFERY built his first experimental Rambler in 1897 in machine shop of his Chicago bicycle factory. In 1902 he and son Charles T. began manufacturing 1-cyl. models for public sale at Kenosha, Wisc., where they had bought Sterling Bicycle Company plant (American Motors Corp.) . . . The first horseless carriage in Minnesota was electric six-seater with high wheels and friction brakes applied to surface of rear tires (below). Note unusual bare bulb headlight. (Minnesota Historical Society).

21

GEORGE B. SELDEN, attorney whose patent No. 549,160 clouded American car manufacturing scene for many years, posed aboard his protoype auto built long after he put his ideas on paper. (The Smithsonian Institution).

AUTOMOGULS...
Men behind the machines

An entire book could be written about the myths of automobile history. Separating fact from the romanticized legends is—and will continue to be—a monumental research task.

The greatest myth of all, of course, has been the all-too-common belief (in the United States) that the automobile is strictly an American institution. True, the historians know better, but the proverbial man-on-the-street somehow lumps the auto right along with hot dogs, apple pie and baseball (also an indirect steal) as totally American achievements.

The truth of the matter, however, is that the New World inventors were really johnny-come-latelys—but once they got going, they made up for lost time. In his excellent book, **Antique Automobiles** (see Bibliography), Anthony Bird brought the historic development into perspective with a single sentence: "Germany may claim to be the birthplace of the modern motor car, France its nursery, England the country where it learned good manners, but nobody can deny that it was in America that the little fellow was taught his real place in the world."

While the saga of the automobile has in general been subject to prose and poetic license, the stories of the men behind the machines have also been embellished by over-zealous writers. And few individuals could match Henry Ford's record as both victim and beneficiary of historical inaccuracies. He has been variously credited as the inventor of America's first auto, the originator of mass-production, creator of industrial demagoguery, and instigator—by indirection—of the workingman's curse: the installment plan. He has been canonized and condemned, lauded and lambasted, idolized and impugned. Fictionalized versions of his life have depicted him as some sort of mechanical mystic, driven from boyhood by the overpowering dream to put the world on wheels.

But Henry Ford needs no embellishment! His accomplishments have provided their own superlatives—and it was an automotive ugly duckling, uneuphoniously labeled the Model T, which established the farmboy-turned-engineer as the symbol of the automoguls who created a new industry, dominant of the national economy.

There is no room here for an encyclopedic tracing of the hundreds of individuals who played important roles in the epic of the automobile. Even total failures contributed to the march of progress—by proving what **wouldn't** work. Some were successes more through quirks of fate, timing and available capital than because of mechanical genius. Still others added

the niceties—like self-starters, clincher tires, anti-knock gas, sliding gear transmissions and magnetic speedometers—which, in turn were improved upon through the years.

In the American chapter of automobiliana, certain names do stand out, however. One of the foremost, of course, is that of George Baldwin Selden, patent attorney, opportunist and not-quite-successful inventor. As early as 1876—the year George Armstrong Custer came out second best at Little Big Horn—Selden, a Civil War veteran, was working on an idea for a gas-operated "road locomotive." He applied for a patent on the basis of his drawings on May 8, 1879. Though he was never able to get his auto into production, more than 16 years later he was granted U.S. Patent No. 549,160 on November 5, 1895, a document which was (to mix a metaphor) a burr under the saddle of the automobile industry for more than a decade.

By the time the patent was granted, John Lambert had operated a gas-mobile in Ohio; Charles R. Black was credited with a Benz-type auto in Indianapolis; the Duryea brothers had been even more successful in Massachusetts; Edgar and Elmer Apperson celebrated the Fourth of July, 1894, in Kokomo, Indiana, by unveiling a car they had built, based on plans conceived by Elwood G. Haynes. That same year Ransom E. Olds had also constructed a workable gas-burning auto.

But Selden had gotten a legal jump on everyone. In 1899 he sold his patent to the Electric Vehicle Company and the Columbia Motor Company of which William C. Whitney was a key figure. Under Whitney's leadership, a number of automobile manufacturers were forced to pay a royalty because they were marketing cars powered by internal combustion engines. There was a legal loophole, however, and Henry Ford took advantage of it.

He refused to join the Association of Licensed Automobile Manufacturers (a group formed to uphold the patent but at the same time to pressure Whitney and his cohorts into reducing the royalty fee). Ultimately, Ford and one of his agents—C. A. Duerr & Company of New York—were sued by the A.L.A.M. The suit dragged on for several years, with a decision in 1909 by the U.S. District Court favoring the patent-holders. Two years later, though, the Court of Appeals made a final ruling: that the Selden patent was valid, but not infringed upon by Ford and other manufacturers. The legal chink was that Selden's patent specified one type of gas engine (a two-cycle Brayton), while another (the four-cycle Otto) was actually used by most auto producers. Ford's attorneys also argued that the Selden design featured the impractical fore-carriage principle—power applied to the front wheels.

By then—1911—the automobile industry had shucked its swaddling clothes. For the first time, securities of automotive companies were listed on the New York Stock Exchange. In the first decade of the twentieth century, the infant industry developed at a fanatic pace. The Ford Motor Company had been formed, and by 1908 had introduced the historic Model T. The Buick Motor Company, the Olds Motor Works, the Cadillac Automobile Company and the Oakland Motor Car Company had already achieved individual success—and had then been combined with other firms by William Crapo Durant into the General Motors Company. Durant, in turn, had lost control of the organization and moved on to another venture, building and selling a new auto, designed by and named for Louis Chevrolet, a French race driver. Another manufacturer-promoter, Benjamin Briscoe, had brought together some 130 different companies to create the United States Motor Car Corporation. Unfortunately, this ambitious combine soon ran into financial difficulties and was doomed to receivership in 1912. Michigan in general, and Detroit in particular, were established as centers of automotive production.

Meanwhile, throughout the nation the general public took to the concept of motorized transportation like moths to Tom Edison's new incandescent lamp. While the moguls invented, merged, maneuvered, sued, counter-sued, promoted, failed or amassed fantastic wealth, curious Americans from Amity, Oregon, to Zook Spur, Iowa, were intrigued enough to unshackle their wallets. Dealerships were set up in livery stables, blacksmith shops and general stores in major cities and the remotest villages. Some of the more mechanically-minded enthusiasts assembled their own vehicles. Others turned to their favorite source of supply—the Sears, Roebuck catalog—to order a Motor Buggy, advertised as so safe that even "a child could run it."

Many of the individuals who contributed in one way or another to the development of the industry have faded into historical oblivion. Others—often because they were memorialized on automobile nameplates—have been treated more kindly by the passing of time. Walter P. Chrysler, Louis Chevrolet, David Dunbar Buick, Ransom E. Olds, Henry Ford, John and Horace Dodge, the White, Mack and Duesenberg brothers were not forgotten. John Mohler Studebaker, John North Willys, Harry C. Stutz, William Crapo Durant, Edwin Ross Thomas, Francis E. and Freelan O. Stanley, Jonathan Dixon Maxwell, Charles W. Nash, James Ward Packard, Thomas B. Jeffery, E. L. Cord, George N. Pierce, Albert Augustus Pope, Howard C. Marmon and others like them have found a niche in automotive annals because their surnames graced the radiators of popular cars of their era.

Only the most avid hobbyists, though, can recall pioneers like H. Bartol Brazier of Philadelphia; J. L. Cato of San Francisco; Dan J. Piscorski of St. Louis, Missouri; W. H. Kiblinger of Auburn, Indiana;

Percy L. Klock of New York; F. J. Fanning of Chicago; C. Clarence Holden of Comanche, Texas; or J. A. Moncrieff of Pawtucket, Rhode Island. They, too, had cars named for them, but for one reason or another, the vehicles failed to achieve continuing acceptance, and cars and creators were ground into the sands of time by the heavy traffic of more successful models.

Not all of the giants and near-giants of the industry were related directly to completed automobiles. There were those whose genius and skills provided the refinements which brought constant improvement to the motoring world. In 1904 Carl Graham Fisher and James A. Allison organized the Prest-O-Lite Company and introduced a new system of acetylene gas headlights. In 1908—the year of the Model T—C. Harold Wills developed the use of vanadium steel for Ford. Concurrently, Charles Y. Knight was perfecting his sleeve-valve engine, and the Fisher brothers founded a company which was to gain rapid fame as a producer of closed auto bodies. The scientific brilliance of Charles Franklin Kettering of the Dayton Engineering Laboratories Company helped bring about such diverse innovations as the electric starter and ethyl gasoline. Harvey S. Firestone, B. F. Goodrich, Arthur W. Grant and other experimenters with rubber struggled to overcome tire deficiencies.

There were men like Edward G. Budd, a young Philadelphia engineer, who is credited with the concept of the all-steel auto body. During the formative years, manufacturers — many of whom had been carriage-makers—used the same techniques and designs they had previously employed for horse-drawn vehicles. The heat of early-day motors, however, caused wood to warp and weakened the glue; rough roads caused joints to give way so that the cars soon creaked and groaned. Budd left a good job to pursue his idea with his own company; in 1912 he finally convinced the Oakland and Hupmobile people to try his all-steel body frames. The next year he received his first large contract from John and Horace Dodge.

Arthur O. Smith, son of a Milwaukee blacksmith and bicycle parts manufacturer, like so many other second-generation industrialists, shifted his interest to the new-fangled horseless carriages. He sold his first pressed steel frames to the Peerless Motor Company early in the new century and when other auto builders became interested, he offered a house and lot to a foreman who could increase his production to twelve frames a day. That's when Henry Ford came to see him—and ordered 10,000 Model T frames for delivery in four months. The challenge was accepted, and by 1921—some 15 years later—the A. O. Smith Corporation was capable of producing Ford's first order in a single day!

The automobile, as it progressed through history, was a product of many hands, of revolutionary concepts and of simple, almost unnoticed upgrading. Countless ideas came from unknown mechanics who achieved neither fame nor monetary reward for their contributions. The ultimate beneficiary was the motorist, whose interest, enthusiasm and money spurred the automoguls to new heights with each passing year.

WILLIAM A. BESSERDICH, co-inventor of four-wheel drive automobile and one of founders of FWD Company. (FWD Corporation).

TILLER-STEERED MOTOR WAG-
ON, with Charles E. Duryea, its
co-builder, at controls, won America's first auto race, sponsored by
Chicago "Times-Herald" on Thanksgiving Day in 1895. J. Frank Duryea
was winning driver. (The Smithsonian Institution).

WALTER P. CHRYSLER (right) was head of Maxwell Motor Corporation in 1924 when he introduced
auto bearing his name. Fred Zeder (left) was one of its key designers. The Chrysler was so successful it
soon caused demise of historic Maxwell known for two decades. (Chrysler Corporation).

26

ARTHUR O. SMITH (right above) posed with Henry Ford in one of the latter's elongated Model Ns. Smith was typical of scores of manufacturers who produced components for early day autos. He accepted Ford's order for 10,000 car frames in 4 months at time when he was still trying to produce 12 a day. (A. O. Smith Corporation) . . . Below is Model 43 Detroit Electric which attracted none other than Henry Ford whose fame and fortune were made with gasoline-driven autos. Earlier he had tinkered with steamer or two. (The Smithsonian Institution).

HARVEY S. FIRESTONE, SR. (shown at left) greeted officers of Army's first transcontinental truck convoy in 1919. At right is Lt. Col. Dwight D. Eisenhower, second in command of caravan. (The Firestone Tire and Rubber Company).

WILLIAM A. BESSERDICH and brother-in-law, Otto Zachow, were young blacksmiths in Clintonville, Wisc., when they built America's first successful four wheel drive motor car in 1909. Their Badger Four Wheel Drive Auto Company was formed on Jan. 9 that year, later "Badger" and "Auto" dropped from title. Firm ultimately switched from cars (like one above) to trucks exclusively. (FWD Corporation).

CHARLES J. GLIDDEN (in white duster), who promoted long-distance reliability runs which did much to publicize early autos. Col. Augustus Post drove White Steamer in 1906 Glidden Tour. (American Automobile Assn.).

DAVID DUNBAR BUICK (left) was successful manufacturer of enameled bathtubs and other plumbing fixtures before he ventured into automobile business in 1902. Year later he produced first Buick car with help of Walter L. Marr. His company was not a success however until William C. Durant bought and reorganized it in 1904. (Photos Buick Motor Div. General Motors Corp.)

LI HUNG CHANG, Chinese statesman, toured Philadelphia in 1905 in gleaming Studebaker. Auto and visiting dignitary were both objects of interest. (The Free Library of Philadelphia).

IN 1908 FISHER BODY COMPANY was established by brothers Fred and Charles who had moved to Detroit from Norwalk, Ohio, to pursue carriage building trade. 2 years later firm became Fisher Body Company and received order from Cadillac for first quantity production of closed bodies—150 units. Shown at this ground-breaking ceremony were 7 brothers—Alfred J. Sr.; Lawrence P.; Charles T. Sr.; Fred J.; William A.; Howard A.; Edward F. (Fisher Body Div., General Motors Corp.).

WILLIAM C. DURANT formed Chevrolet Motor Company by combining Little Motor Company and Republic Motor Company. Shown here (standing) Durant, William Little and Louis Chevrolet. In first production model built by new firm were Mr. and Mrs. Clifford Durant. (Chevrolet Div., General Motors Corp.).

CARL BENZ successfully tested his first gasoline engine auto at Mannheim, Germany, in 1885, is photographed here with Daughter Carla in this Benz Victoria which he built in 1893. He and fellow German, Gottlieb Daimler, were instrumental in developing internal combustion engine and adapting it to motor car. (Pennsylvania Historical and Museum Commission).

NAME OF RANSOM E. OLDS who built his first gas-engine auto in 1894, was perpetuated in Oldsmobile and Reo. As manager of Olds Motor Vehicle Company he was authorized in memo below to build firm's first car in 1897. Note editing of word "perfect". (Photos Oldsmobile Div. General Motors Corp.).

LOUIS CHEVROLET (below), intrepid race driver from France, was also designer and mechanic. He conceived auto which was to bear his name in 1911. William Durant, forced out of General Motors Corporation he had formed, saw the Chevrolet as a car to challenge Model T dominance. (Detroit Public Library Automotive History Collection).

HORACE AND JOHN DODGE (in rear seat photo left) were wealthy manufacturers of components for Olds Motor Works, then Ford Motor Company, before they introduced their own auto. First Dodge was delivered to them on Nov. 14, 1914 (Dodge News Photo).

CHARLES METZ (below—with cap standing by car), first organized Waltham, Massachusetts, manufacturing company to make bicycles. Later his Orient Buckboard was designed specifically for postal service and friction-drive Metz 22 for low-priced auto market. Team of 3 Metz cars won 1913 Glidden Tour with perfect score. (Chas. Lytle Collection).

CHARLES F. KETTERING, pliers and screwdriver genius of automotive industry, was one of founders of Dayton Engineering Laboratories Company (Delco) in 1909. Here he makes personal adjustment on engine in 1913; 8 years later (shown second from right) he participated in Delco test caravan. His greatest contribution was electric self-starter introduced in 1912. (Photos Delco Products Div. General Motors Corp.).

DEVELOPMENT OF SERVICEABLE TIRES was vital to continuing success of automobile. One pioneer was Harvey S. Firestone, pictured with a company test driver in 1917, 17 years after he came to Akron, Ohio, to seek fortune in rubber industry. (The Firestone Tire and Rubber Company) . . . Below are his long-time friends, Thomas Edison and Henry Ford, vacationing together at Iron Mountain, Mich. An inveterate practical joker, Ford must have had some bit of whimsey in mind with six-shooter and bandana. (Ford Motor Company).

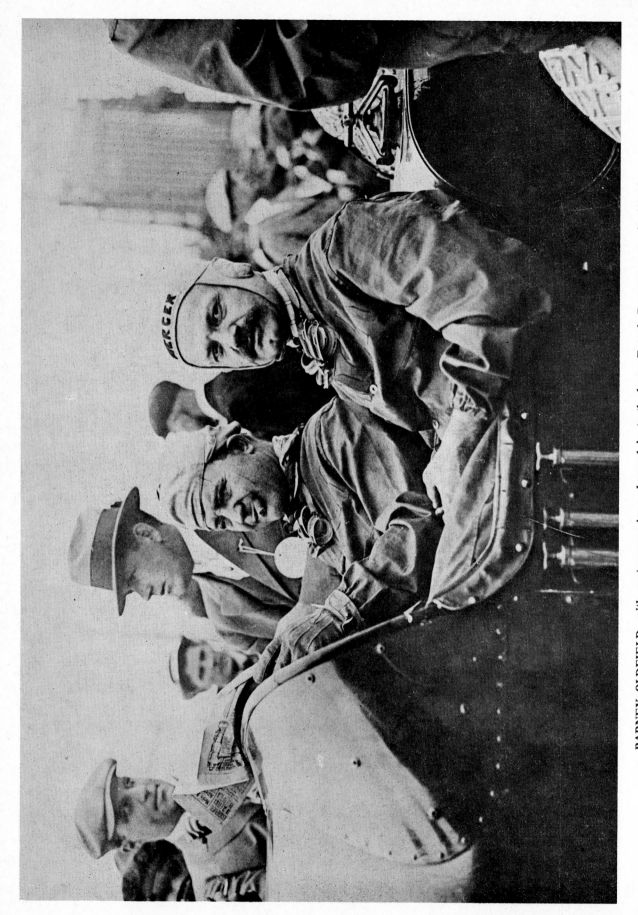

BARNEY OLDFIELD, with customary cigar clamped in teeth drove French Peugeot racer in 1913 in Indianapolis 500. His name became synonymous with speed in motoring's early days. His racing career lasted 17 years. (Firestone Tire and Rubber Company).

ENDURANCE RACE preparations in 1900s. Below left, 1911 Maxwell; below right, 1-cyl. Reo in 1911.

MODEL T AND MODEL TEAM depict all-too-common practice in era of minimal roads and mechanical undependability. (Texaco Archives).

OLD DOBBIN
gets a final horse laugh

The ultimate height of personal indignity occurred regularly during the pioneer days of the automobile. It usually happened in much the same way.

The peacock-proud owner of a new horseless carriage would load his family into the machine while the neighbors ogled with envy. Invariably the budding automobilist would over-dramatize the ritual of donning his gloves, checking his equipment and cranking the engine into cacaphonous action. Then, with heads held high, driver and passengers would begin their baptismal trek into the country, beaming with self-satisfaction—and taking a route, of course, which would "just happen" to go by the homes of the "right people." If ever an event qualified as the thril!-of-a-lifetime, that was it!

Unfortunately, such joyous beginnings didn't always have a happy ending.

Somewhere along the way, the tiny engine would start to cough and sputter. The confident driver would assure his passengers that there was nothing to worry about. However, when the mechanical hiccoughing continued, his assuredness would waiver—and when the motor finally died, the ego-deflated new owner literally suffered the pangs of the damned.

Then—when no amount of tinkering or coaxing would revive the recalcitrant engine—the humiliating trek to the nearest farm house would take place. Most likely the farmer would add to the mental anguish by making several uncomplimentary remarks about "them new fangled contraptions," but with an air of stability, he would harness his team and hitch it to the front of the ailing auto. A special dirge should have been written to accompany the homeward trip of a horse-drawn horseless carriage. Gone were the proud airs; mother and daughters blushed appropriately; young sons usually enjoyed the experience; but father was on the verge of an apoplectic fit.

And old Dobbin—as slow, expensive and old-fashioned as he was—got a final horse laugh!

It is somehow appropriate that through the years "horse-power" has continued to be a measurement of an automobile's mechanical muscle. Certainly an animal which has contributed so much to civilization deserves some lasting identification with the vehicle by which it was so unceremoniously dumped from public favor. The horse was more than just replaced; he was caught up in a competitive situation which saw him maligned by copywriters, ridiculed by a

LOOK OF ABJECT DISGUST was appropriate at time like this! Fortunately replacement of horse was transitional so there were plenty of plodding oat-burners available to pull floundering motorists out of muck. (Portland Cement Association).

new breed of high-powered merchants called auto dealers and even attacked by health authorities who saw in the motor car the end of manure heaps, disease-toting flies and assorted other vermin.

The latter argument against the age-old servant of man was particularly telling. Anyone down-wind from a livery stable took little convincing that the horse had an aromatic drawback. And it was easy for an advertising soothsayer to win over a populace plagued with an obvious need for sticky flypaper, patented insect traps and foul-smelling sprays. In the early years of the twentieth century, the public was in the mood for progress, and a slow-footed oat-burner simply did not fit.

There were some, though, who envisioned that the motor car wouldn't be all health and happiness, either. In 1904 the **Review of Reviews** warned:

> Granted that the horse is not cleanly and that his hoofs make a noise, but about the automobile? The exhaust and cinders from a steam truck, the noisy and evil smelling exhaust of certain gasoline cars, the dripping of oil, the difficulty of cleaning a storage battery . . . these are some of the objections that might be pointed out.

The economic argument was hammered home by the automobile publicists. They continually echoed the refrain that each horse in the U.S. required the production of five acres of land and 20 man-days of care per year. Before 1900 Ransom E. Olds, writing in **Scientific American,** took an indirect swing at the horse when he described his new steam carriage: ". . . it never kicks or bites, never tires on long runs, and never sweats in hot weather. It does not require care in the stable and only eats while on the road."

The stories of runaways, overturned buggies and other equine accidents were dramatized and widely disseminated. In 1899 **The Automobile Magazine** recited a litany of horse-related tragedies:

"In Philadelphia a young man was driving a cart. A piece of paper blew beneath the horse's feet. The animal ran and the young man was thrown out and killed."

"At Maumee, Ohio, the sting of a wasp made a horse run away, throwing out a man with his two little daughters."

"At Cynthiana, Kentucky . . . the explosion of a giant fire-cracker frightened a horse and caused the death of three of the four occupants of a carriage."

"In Chicago a lady and gentlemen were out driving. The lady opened her parasol . . . A runaway, upset and serious hurts followed."

"In Little Rock, Arkansas, a prominent citizen was driving with his wife. The horse took fright at some passing bicycles, the lady was thrown out and killed by the crushing of her skull against an electric light post."

Of the 476 accidents analyzed by the magazine, only two were caused because the horses involved were frightened by automobiles. This statistical whitewash, of course, was supposed to refute the common plaint that motor cars were scaring otherwise docile horses right out their whiffletrees.

In a turn-of-the-century treatise entitled "How the Horse Runs Amuck," Sylvester Baxter reached into his bag of adjectives and adverbs to propagandize thusly:

It is quite natural that the horse should have a nature so unbalanced mentally; evolved, as he is, from an ancestor who was one of the most timid of wild animals, possessing no weapons of offence or defence, and therefore finding his only safety in flight. He had ever to be on the alert, with his keen senses of perception ever tense; ready to urge him into a mad gallop at the slightest movement, or rustling of a leaf, which, perhaps, might betray the neighborhood of some lurking and terrible beast of prey about to spring upon him and tear his life out with lacerating claws or teeth. It is no wonder, therefore, that at any unaccustomed sight, noise, touch or motion the horse of today . . . should still be seized with an ungovernable terror that expresses itself in a mad onward rush whose frightful power is fraught with destruction for everything about him.

The anti-horse haranguers, always looking for new ammunition, made the most of a vicious heat wave which hit New York City in July of 1911. An estimated 1,200 horses dropped dead in the streets because of the scorching temperatures, and it was quickly pointed out that motor cars and trucks continued to function without difficulty or detriment to the health of the populace.

Occasionally there would be a note of rebuttal or a sentimental rejoinder, but in spite of the fact that there were some 25 million horses in the country in 1912, Old Dobbin was "out" and the automobile was "in," socially and economically. William Allen White, the famed editor of Emporia, Kansas, was not entirely ready to give up on the gallant old four-legged steed which had always been good enough before the advent of the auto. About his favorite horse, Allen penned:

> He makes no claim to speed, but his carburetor always works, and while he has but two cylinders, he brings his guests back in one piece and leaves them at home rather than downtown at the undertaker's to be assembled by total strangers into their aliquot parts.

The transition from a centuries-old form of land transportation to a totally different concept was not easy—nor was it possible to achieve in a matter of a year or two. The horse, after all, was an important factor in the national economy. Feed and veterinary bills amounted to millions of dollars annually. According to **The Chicago Tribune** in 1915, horseshoes that year required enough iron to build 60,000 motor cars. Harness makers, buggy-whip companies, carriage builders, livery stable operators, blacksmiths, an army of street cleaners, wheelwrights and even hitching post manufacturers were all affected by the technological development. They either had to re-tool and adapt to the new industry or face the realities of a gradually declining business.

The demands of World War I—while they further spurred the production of motor vehicles—also protracted the need for horses and mules. With the Armistice, however, came the final turning point, and from then on it was a downhill run for Old Dobbin—not to oblivion, of course, because there will always be race tracks, rodeos, show rings, riding clubs and Wild West movies—but to a miniscule role in transportation and agriculture.

The horseless carriage reigned supreme! And the carriageless horse retired to greener pastures . . . or took the long, sad journey to the nearest glue factory.

MOE AND MARY plod valiantly toward oblivion as era of tank trucks was coming up fast behind them. (The Free Library of Philadelphia).

HENRY B. JAY, simultaneously president of Packard Motor Car Company and Lincoln Highway Association was no doubt spurred to further action in promoting roads after being stuck in this Nebraska mud hole (right) enroute to Pan-Pacific Exposition in 1915. (Portland Cement Assn.).

DIRT ROADS which sufficed for horse and buggy were soon gouged to pieces by heavier, speedier automobiles. Youngster shown (below left) was born at end of one mode of transportation and beginning of another (Wash. State Dept. of Highways) . . . When water holes got deep enough to short out battery or fill carburetor, horses and mules plodded on (below right) while motorists sat in dejection. Obvious answer was to improve roads and growing army of auto owners devoted efforts to that end. (Minnesota Historical Society).

WHEN AUTOMOBILES AP-
PROACHED, skittish horses had to
be pulled off road to prevent accidents or runaways. Some state laws
required motorist to stop car while
horses or mules passed by . . . all
part of transition from one age to
a n o t h e r. (American Automobile
Assn.).

PHOTOGRAPHER MADE HIS POINT (above) in this obviously contrived picture. There was something romantic about a horse and carriage but lure of motor car was too great and autoless swain was soon left in dust and exhaust fumes. (Library of Congress) . . . Below left, a quizzical saddle horse looks over Dodge touring car, one of many sent to Mexican border in 1916-17 to aid military pursuit of Pancho Villa. Young Lt. George Smith Patton, Jr. used 3 such cars to rout nest of bandits out of adobe fortress. (Chrysler Corporation) . . . In evolution of transportation, animals and mechanical power vied for a time on same job (below right). Invariably motor car won out. Switching from reins to steering wheels proved difficult for some teamsters, who could not restrain their "whoas." (Standard Oil Co. of Calif.)

INTERNATIONAL TRUCK and four-horse stagecoach represented old and new (above) in inter-city transport. For a time both modes of travel had to be accommodated by supporting industries; livery stables and garages, oat raisers and gasoline peddlers, harness makers and auto parts suppliers. Demands of motor vehicles soon surpassed needs of horse however. . . . International Harvester Auto-Wagon (below) was high-wheeled, hard-tired pioneer version of pickup truck. Doleful Dobbin behind symbolized passing of an era. (Photos International Harvester Company).

THIS CLASSIC PHOTOGRAPH epitomized period of automotive development when Old Dobbin was still important asset—especially for motorist who ventured too far from town. Some farmers were glad to help out just to see a motor car up close. Others were scornful and charged healthy fees for towing. (American Automobile Assn.)

NEAR CHESTER, VIRGINIA (opposite bottom), in 1914, a king-size touring car was subjected to indignities of mule rescue. Weather governed shape of roads and in most parts of country sudden rain could trap a wandering motorist in a quagmire. (U.S. Bureau of Public Roads).

MOST PIONEER MOTORISTS stored their autos during winter months, not only because of operation difficulties but because of snow-clogged roads. Antifreeze, winter oils, efficient heaters and other cold weather necessities were due to come. (Mich. State Dept. of Highways)

BUICK MOTOR COMPANY proudly boasted in 1904 that this Model B had traveled "fast as the winds" from Detroit to Lansing, covering 102 miles in just 217 minutes. (Buick Motor Div. General Motors Corp.)

SURVIVAL...
of the Fittest and Fleetest

From the very beginning, automobile builders and owners have seemingly had an obsession to prove that their vehicles are better, bigger, faster, more powerful, possessed of greater stamina, more economical, more efficient, quieter or classier than all others.

For that reason they devised races, exhibitions, endurance tests and other performance events to show what their cars could do.

At first, it was a case of convincing a skeptical public that the horseless carriage was more than just a freak or a passing fancy. It was a period when car-versus-horse was the main theme. Afterwards, when it became apparent that the automobile was on the scene for posterity, the competition quickly took the form of manufacturer-against-manufacturer.

There is apparently some factor in the makeup of a human being which instills in him a gnawing desire to beat everyone else across a finish line—whether he's afoot, on horseback or at a steering tiller. No sooner had the automobile become a working reality when the racing bug manifested itself among inventors and pioneer owners. Again, the motorists of France got the jump. On July 22, 1894, 13 steam and 8 gas-driven vehicles participated in a 78-mile reliability run from Paris to Rouen. It was not supposed to be a race as such, but the natural inclination to crown a winner was most evident. Though his six-wheeled "Steam Horse" had to be dug out of a potato patch, Count De Dion was first to reach Rouen, and he was promptly recognized as unofficial victor in the non-race. So much interest was aroused among French motor enthusiasts that they established the Automobile Club of France (the first such organization in the world) and started making plans for a Paris-Bordeaux-Paris speed run. The event took place in June of 1895 with a heterogeneous collection of entries ranging from mammoth steam vans to motorized bicycles. First to conquer the 732-mile course was Emile Levassor, who piloted this two-cylinder Panhard-Levassor for more than 48 hours without a relief driver.

In America, the French event attracted enough attention to start a few promotion wheels turning. The outcome was an announcement by the Chicago **Times-Herald** that the newspaper would sponsor, on November 1, 1895, a horseless carriage race from Chicago to Waukegan and return. Even with the lure of a gold medal and $5,000 in prize money, though, there were not enough operating entries at starting time to make the effort worthwhile. In a so-called "consolation" contest on November 2, four cars managed to get underway. Unfortunately, none of the vehicles were able to complete the required mileage, and no winner was declared.

Publisher H. H. Kohlsaat of the **Times-Herald** was a persistent man, however, and on Thanksgiving Day (November 28), a half dozen autos sputtered out of Lincoln Park in quest of victory. They included a Duryea Motor Wagon; an imported Benz entered by H. Mueller & Sons of Decatur, Illinois; a "Rogers Machine" representing R. H. Macy & Company of New York; a "Motor Drag" sponsored by the De la Vergne Refrigerating Machine Company of New York; a Sturgis Electric Motocycle from Chicago; and a Morris & Salom Electrobat from Philadelphia.

A slushy snowfall made the going extremely difficult. The two electric cars were quick to fold; the Macy entry skidded on a streetcar track and slammed into the rear of a horse-drawn tram. The De la Vergne representative ended up in a snow drift, but J. Frank Duryea tillered his historic auto over the 55-mile abbreviated course well ahead of the only other finisher. That was the German Benz driven alternately by Oscar and Frederick Mueller, sons of the owner. The physical strain was too much for the Mueller brothers, though, so Charles Brady King—the umpire assigned to the car and who was later to be the first man to operate an auto in Detroit—finally took over the controls for the final miles. Most historians now accept this rescheduled event as the first successful auto race in the U. S.

And that, of course, was just the beginning. On September 7, 1896, a Rikker Electric won the nation's inaugural closed track competition at Narragansett Park, Rhode Island. It was, by eyewitness accounts, a boring experience, as a Morris & Salom Elctrobat took second and three gas-powered Duryeas were the also-rans. Two other Duryeas were disqualified. Earlier in the year, though, Frank Duryea had won his second consecutive victory in the Cosmopolitan Race from New York City to Irvington-on-the-Hudson and return. The racing ardor increased with the addition of more and more autos. Informal road races grew out of the simple challenge, "my car is faster than your car"—with appropriate side bets. Occasionally these contests had to be "bootlegged" somewhere out in the country because of stringent speed laws.

William K. Vanderbilt, Jr., who drove a Mercedes racer to a new speed record of 92.3 miles per hour on January 27, 1904 (beating the 91.37 mark established by Henry Ford in his "999" earlier that month), instituted the socially popular Vanderbilt Cup Race the following fall. A Panhard-Levassor from France won the inaugural trophy on a 30-mile triangular course on Long Island. Not until 1908 did an American-made car—a Locomobile—capture the Vanderbilt prize. That was also the year in which road racing reached its apex with the sponsorship by the French newspaper **Le Matin** of a New York-to-Paris race the hard way—via Pocatello, Vladivostok, Tomsk, Omsk and St. Petersburg. The winner was an American-made, steam-driven Thomas Flyer which had traveled 13,341 miles under its own power, plus an additional 8,659 miles by water, all within 170 days, from February 12 to July 30. A three-ton German Protos actually reached Paris first, but because it had been shipped by rail across the Rocky Mountains and had skipped Japan altogether, it was penalized and awarded second prize.

Another cross-country race was started by President William Howard Taft when he pressed a telegraph key in Washington, D. C., which signalled "go" to five cars waiting in New York City. The date was June 1, 1909, and the goal was the Alaska-Yukon-Pacific Exposition in Seattle, Washington. Two stripped-down Fords, a six-cylinder Acme, a massive Shawmut built in Stoneham, Massachusetts, and a foreign-made Italia followed the pace car (a Model K Ford) westward. A sixth starter—a Stearns—didn't get underway until five days later, and then only lasted for about 25 miles. (Selden-licensed manufacturers refused to sanction the contest.)

It was another wild junket, fraught with problems of geography, mechanics and weather. Rain, hail, broken axles, punctured tires and washed-out bridges dogged the contestants. The Shamut became mired in quicksand; the Italia was nudged by a Union Pacific train while crossing the Missouri on a railroad trestle; one of the Ford teams ran out of gas in the desert and wasted a day "hitch-hiking" by train to the nearest town for a re-supply. Ultimately all five of the original starters made it to Seattle, though the Italia arrived by train from Cheyenne, Wyoming, where it had broken down. The No. 2 Ford team of Bert W. Scott, driver, and C. J. Smith, mechanic, claimed the trophy and prize money awarded by Robert Guggenheim after a flurry of protests. It was good publicity for the A-Y-P, and Henry Ford likewise made the most of it during his period of legal hassling with the Association of Licensed Automobile Manufacturers.

The desire for more and more speed, to set and to break records, resulted almost immediately in the designing of two different types of automobiles. There were the stock cars, for family, business and pleasure uses; there were also the specially built vehicles for time trials and track competition. The latter included Henry Ford's historic "999" which early in the new century brought notoriety not only to the builder but to an ex-cycle racer named Berner Eli (Barney) Oldfield. At the same time Oldsmobile was represented by a unique stripped-down speedster called the

"Pirate," while Alexander Winton's "Bullet" was another formidable challenger. In 1906 a streamlined Stanley Steamer known as the "Rocket" was piloted to a then-fantastic world record speed of 127.66 miles-per-hour at Ormond Beach (later known as Daytona Beach) Florida, by Fred Marriott, the first human being to be clocked officially at more than two miles-a-minute.

Meanwhile, the non-professionals were having races of their own, less publicized perhaps, but certainly not lacking in imagination. In 1909—the same year in which the Indianapolis Speedway was established—a group of Pierre, South Dakota, auto owners staged an unusual motor Olympiad in the tiny capital city. A Kissel Kar won the hill-coasting contest with comparative ease—but the big attraction was the potato race, a crowd-pleasing test of skill, daring-do, physical agility and automotive performance. A potato was placed on the curb at half-block intervals along the race course. The event itself was a wild stop-and-go melee as drivers dashed from spud to spud, braked their cars, jumped out and grabbed a tuber, then leaped back in to roar on to the next vegetable cache. In a screeching, rubber-burning performance. Dr. T. F. Riggs in his scarlet Hupmobile roadster was a popular winner.

While speed matches were the choice of one group of pioneer motorists, another favored endurance trials or reliability runs. These ranged from individual efforts to festive inter-city tours with dozens of cars involved. Alexander Winton recognized the promotion value of such city-to-city journeys as early as 1897 when he sent one of his autos from Cleveland to New York in ten days. Two years later he made the same trip himself in 47 hours and 37 minutes driving time. It was in 1901, though, that an organized tour from New York to Buffalo (prematurely cut short in Rochester because of the death of President McKinley) added a new dimension to auto travel.

The excitement and comradery of a long-distance jaunt appealed to the early-day motorists, and for the next dozen years mass junkets were quite commonplace. In 1903 some 34 automobiles participated in an endurance run from New York to Pittsburgh. It was a rain-bedeviled excursion which took more than a week. The event became known as the "Mud Lark," and the drivers involved formed an organization with that name. Next year the American Automobile Association sponsored a pioneer pilgrimage from New York City to the Louisiana Purchase Exposition in St. Louis. It was a disorganized affair marked by frazzled nerves and a few short tempers; still, the event was successful enough so that one of the participants—Charles J. Glidden—proposed a series of extended cavalcades which were to bear his name (see Page 73).

From one end of the country to the other the horseless carriage craze began to affect the whole populace. If you couldn't own one, you could stand on the curb and gawk at the fortunate elite showing off their runabouts, Stanhopes, phaetons and broughams. High society took to "automobilism" with great delight, and as a climax to the summer season of 1899 at Newport, Rhode Island, a parade of flower-bedecked motor cars had an entry list which ranged through the "400" from the Astors to the Vanderbilts. The colorful event started a trend of floral tours in other cities.

That same year the Automobile Club of America was founded with one of its purposes being the expansion of interest in motor vehicles. In November of 1900 the organization sponsored the first National Automobile Show in Madison Square Garden. Some 48,000 spectators marveled at the wide variety of cars (more than 40 different makes) priced from $280 to $4,000; they were especially fascinated by a hill-climbing demonstration of Mobile Steamers on a 200-foot ramp built to the Garden roof. People everywhere wanted to see the new automobiles, to touch the shiny tonneaus and—thrill of thrills!—maybe even to ride in one of them. The Barnum & Bailey Circus had capitalized on this magnetic appeal as early as 1896 by including a Duryea Motor Wagon in its pre-show parade.

In 1899 Freelan O. Stanley demonstrated the power of the Stanley Steamer by driving one up Mt. Washington in New Hampshire. The following year John Brisben Walker drove another steamer to the top of Pikes Peak. The auto promoters were ever on the alert for new heights to conquer, new roads to explore and new customers to impress. Autos were driven up church and courthouse steps; gasoline economy runs were instituted; magazine and newspaper advertisements began to feature claims and counter-claims of scores of manufacturers.

Copywriters called the jaunty Yale "the Beau Brummel of the road." They proclaimed widely that "every Pope-Toledo is tested to do a mile in one minute flat before leaving the factory." Builders of electrics and air-cooled models argued the advantages of "no water to freeze." The Flint Automobile Company's Roadster had "a muffler that muffles" and 18 coats of paint. The 1910 Cadillac Thirty boasted 112

parts "accurace to the one-thousandth of an inch."

Interchangeability was proved in 1909 in England when three Cadillacs were disassembled and the parts literally mixed in a blanket. Using only wrenches and screw drivers, mechanics rebuilt all three cars from the conglomerate mess—and the trio of autos proceeded to complete a 500-mile test run with no trouble.

As early as 1909 the hucksters were promoting multiple ownership: "If you can afford to maintain two cars—one of them should by all means be a Hupmobile." In 1908 an advertisement in **Munsey's Magazine** featured a theme which was prophetic of America's later-day Suburbia: "The Sears is the car for the business man who has tired of home life in a congested neighborhood and yearns for a cottage in the suburbs for his family." The H. H. Babcock Company of Watertown, New York, raised a note of snob appeal with the claim that its product was "built only for those willing to pay for quality and workmanship. If you are looking for an automobile at buggy price, don't write us." In 1902 the Olds Motor Works also adopted the negative twist:

> You can pay more money for an automobile and get more smoke, smell, noise, trouble and profanity than we can offer you. If you are anxious to experiment, don't send for our catalog.

The first decade of the twentieth century was a period of transition, of trial-and-error, of success and failure. Dozens of manufacturers emerged with a flourish and disappeared with hardly a ripple in the industrial mainstream. Lack of capital, poor business judgment, ineffective promotion and salesmanship were all factors involved in the collapse of various short-lived companies. Often, however, those auto builders who hung on and grew larger owed their continued existence to an age-old principle: the survival of the fittest—and the fleetest!

AN AUTO THAT WOULDN'T RUN made no friends for pioneer manufacturers. It was particularly embarrassing for new owners to chug proudly out of town—then return afoot, pushing and tugging. (Denver Public Library Western Collection).

SECOND TRANSCONTINENTAL RUN (top) was made in 1903 by Tom Fetch in 1-cyl. Packard dubbed "Old Pacific." He left San Francisco June 20 and arrived in New York 53 days later. In Nevada desert Fetch used umbrella to protect self and car. (Harrah's Automobile Collection) . . . The Dodge brothers—John and Horace—were particularly conscious of their auto's performance, so built wooden rack and incline (above) next to their plant at Hamtramck, Mich., to test each new vehicle before it went to dealer. (Dodge Div. Chrysler Motors Corp.)

IN 1903 L. L. WHITMAN (above with mustache) and Eugene Hammond completed 3d San Francisco-New York trip in auto history. It took them from July 6 to Sept. 17 to conquer trackless prairies, unbridged streams and other geographical barriers. Their auto was curved-dash Oldsmobile. (Oldsmobile Div. General Motors Corp.) . . . Promotion-minded automobile manufacturers sought every possible means to show their products superior. This publicity shot (below) demonstrated strength of door hinges on 1926 Essex. (American Motors Corporation).

THE RACING OBSESSION caused development of special cars designed specifically for purpose. Operation of Indianapolis Speedway in 1909 and other closed-track courses helped create organized sport of informal country road races. (Photos opposite page J. I. Case Company) . . . Both formal and spur-of-the-moment auto races were delight of early day motorists (above and right below). There were so many makes and models, plus 3 major power sources to create special challenge. (Photos Minnesota Historical Society).

HENRY FORD had brief fling at race track. He drove his famous "999" (left above) in 1902 before Barney Oldfield took it over. Earlier he beat Alexander Winton at Grosse Point, Mich. in car designed by Oliver E. Barthel with Ford's assist. Barthel was probably second man in this weathered old photo, crouching behind dash to keep gas feed adjusted. (Ford Motor Company) . . . Above center is stripped-down two-man Pope-Toledo which won Kenwood Hill climbing contest in Minneapolis in 1907. Such events were popular in all parts of country. (Minnesota Historical Society).

EVERY MOUNTAIN IN U.S. with anything resembling road was climbed by pioneer motorists. Pikes Peak in Colorado was special challenge. Fred A. Trinkle (right above) made it to Summit House in 1908 with Brush Runabout. (Denver Public Library Western Collection) . . . As Olds Motor Works was mass-producing famous curved-dash Runabout, it also startled automotive world with the "Pirate" (below), unique speedster, which in 1903 at Ormond Beach, Fla., established new record for measured mile in less than one minute. It was not a commercial product but helped build the Olds' record. (Oldsmobile Div. General Motors Corp.).

OVER HILL AND DALE, across the country and through the woods they went—all types of autos being touted as the best on the market. The 1916 Hudson (above) made a transcontinental run; the 1922 Oldsmobile (below) participated in a tour around Lake Michigan in behalf of better roads. (Top) American Motors Corporation; (bottom) Oldsmobile Division, General Motors Corporation.

"MY CAR CAN BEAT YOURS" was an oral gauntlet thrown by many knights of road. On quiet Sunday mornings, or any other time, races were bound to occur. Admittedly such contests on public roads were dangerous and local laws finally curtailed them . . . Below, parade of 1910 Hudson roadsters, emphasizing fun of guy-'n-gal outing; novel promotion for one-year-old company. Auto's name came from J. L. Hudson, wealthy Detroit merchant who provided capital for venture. (Top, the Smithsonian Institution; center, Ford Motor Company; bottom, American Motors Corp.).

CLIMBING CHURCH or courthouse steps was considered a reliable performance test for pioneer auto. It may have been reasonable assumption because in some rockier areas of nation, roads had about that much pitch and bounce. (Minnesota Historical Society).

BEGINNING WITH first National Auto Show in New York City's Madison Square Garden in 1900, motor car exhibits were exciting, crowd-luring events. One photographed here (left) was in Denver's Civic Center in 1920. (Denver Public Library Western Col.).

MANY NEWSPAPERS sponsored tours, races and other automobile events in formative age of industry. People were curious about motor cars so they made legitimate news. In Minneapolis (opposite top) the "Journal" used this vintage Winton for demonstration runs in 1904. (Minnesota Historical Society). Manufacturers staged tests and demonstrations of every kind. In 1922 this Oldsmobile Six (opposite bottom) went across the country in a single gear to prove something or other. Low, second and reverse gears were removed. (Oldsmobile Div. General Motors Corp.).

ODYSSEY OF
OLD SCOUT and OLD STEADY

There was something magic about a transcontinental race in the embryonic days of motoring. A cross-country tour attracted national attention and brought considerable publicity to the autos and individuals involved.

In 1903 Dr. H. Nelson Jackson of Burlington, Vermont, and a 22-year-old mechanic, Sewell K. Crocker of Tacoma, Washington, left San Francisco on May 23 in a two-cylinder chain-driven Winton. Sixty-three days later they were in New York City after completing the first coast-to-coast automobile trip in history, and for which Doctor Jackson won a $50 bet. Twice more the nation was spanned by car that year. Tom Fetch drove a single-cylinder Packard between the same two cities and beat the Jackson-Crocker record by ten days. Later in the summer it took L. L. Whitman and E. T. Hammond ten weeks to shepherd a curved-dash Oldsmobile from the Pacific to the Atlantic.

The excitement generated by such automotive odysseys was well recognized by industry publicists. Wherever a sign-bedecked tour car stopped—especially in the hinterlands—crowds would gather, and the growing desire to own a motor car would be instilled in a few more potential customers. That's why the Olds Motor Works was most receptive to an idea in 1905 to have its automobiles featured in a transcontinental race from New York City to Portland, Oregon. Not only would it be good publicity for the vehicles, but the long trip would focus attention on the roads of America and possibly bring some improvements. Both results, of course, would be good for Oldsmobile.

Portland was the site of the Lewis and Clark Centennial Exposition that year, and the National Good Roads Association also selected the Rose City for its convention. James W. Abbott, special agent for the Rocky Mountain Division of the U. S. Office of Public

OLD SCOUT AND OLD STEADY had only minor troubles in New York-Chicago phase of journey. Above photo taken in northern Indiana. Opposite, the two toboggan-nosed Oldsmobiles were poised at Columbus Circle in New York City, May 8, 1905, ready to begin cross-country dash. (Oldsmobile Div., General Motors Corp.).

Roads, proposed the race as a promotion gimmick for both events; the suggestion won ready approval in a year of considerable national prosperity and optimism.

Selected for the competition were two 1905 curved-dash Oldsmobiles, doughty little tiller-steered runabouts powered by one-cylinder, seven-horsepower engines. To tell them apart, one was dubbed Old Scout and the other Old Steady, the names being painted on the toboggan-like noses of the frail-appearing, open-air motor-buggies. Manning Old Scout was a team composed of Dwight B. Huss and Milford Wigle; Percy F. Megargel and Barton Stanchfield were assigned to Old Steady. Huss and Megargel had both gained valuable experience in the 1904 New York-to-St. Louis tour; but they were to learn much, much more before they trundled into the shadow of Mt. Hood almost 4,000 miles away.

On the morning of May 8 a curious crowd gathered at Columbus Circle in front of Harrold's Motor Car Company, distributor of Oldsmobiles and Pierce-Arrows. Derby-topped dandies and knicker-clad youngsters gawked excitedly; there was a frantic, last-minute checking of equipment and supplies; then, promptly at 9:30 a.m., the two cars were side-cranked into action and the race was on!

In reality, until well past the half-way point, the journey was more of a tour than an actual race. The two cars left New York together, putt-putted up the Hudson to Albany, then headed westward through Syracuse, Buffalo, Erie and Cleveland. The roads—such as they were—held up well and mileage was good. As a matter of fact, only a limited encounter with hub-deep mud in northern Ohio marred the first week of the excursion. There were the usual stops for minor repairs, of course, tires to be patched and gasoline to be found. Service stations were non-existent, so the location of fuel required a certain amount of sleuthing. It began to appear that the expected gruelling race would be just a jolly jaunt across the nation when the two vehicles pulled into Chicago in only seven days of relatively uneventful driving. The big problems, however, all lay ahead!

Spring rains changed the entire complexion of the trip west of the Windy City. The dirt roads across Illinois became a quagmire as the tiny under-powered cars sloshed and splattered from one mud hole to the next. It took 17½ hours to travel the 64 miles from Chicago to Geneseo. The occupants of the autos were virtually unrecognizable in a cocoon of black goo; even Wigle's mustache was encrusted, as if he'd just come in first in a mud-pie eating contest. Periodically the cars had to be stopped so that the wheels could be cleaned off sufficiently to see the wooden spokes.

The Mississippi River was crossed at Davenport, and the Iowa gumbo took up where the Illinois black muck left off. The rains continued to come, and the mud got worse. It would pack up around the radiator coils, and engines would heat up. It was no longer possible to tell which car was Old Scout and which was Old Steady without digging through a layer of sticky clay. The Skunk River bottom proved particularly formidable as a motoring barrier. There were times when one or the other of the cars would be stalled in the rain-saturated lowlands with all four wheels out of sight, battery shorted out and carburetor full of water. Then it was no longer a matter of driving. Out would come the trusty block-and-tackle and the auto would be winched forward from one tree or telegraph pole to the next.

Somehow or other, though, the two plucky Oldsmobiles made it to Omaha. There—like the '49ers and Oregon Trail commuters of another generation—the travelers made special preparations to challenge the rugged expanse of the West. The runabouts didn't have the carrying capacity of a covered wagon, but as best they could, the two teams loaded down their vehicles with extra gas tanks, water containers, special sand tires, cooking utensils, a food supply, firearms and ammunition. Then they chugged out into the Nebraska sand hills.

At this point, the two-car tour ended and the race really began. Old Scout pulled away from Old Steady, and the vehicles were never together again until they finally reached Portland. East of the Missouri River, bridges and culverts were fairly adequate under normal weather conditions; as the competitors pressed farther into the wide open spaces, structural refinements ranged from minimal to non-existent. Most streams had to be forded, and once again the block-and-tackle became a most valuable piece of equipment.

There were other complications, too. In Wyoming a May snowstorm provided a chilling experience. In the same state another storm sent the motorists scurrying for cover as the earth was blanketed two inches deep with hailstones. Sage brush battered the radiators, and sand tires were necessary to cross the desert wastelands. But the two cars plunged on—past curious, unbelieving Indians; across the tire-shredding lava beds of Idaho; through choking alkali dust in central Oregon and on to the Cascade Mountains, the last major barrier before the finish line.

By this time Old Scout was well ahead of Old Steady; only a disaster could have changed the shape of the race—and the disaster almost occurred. Dwight Huss and Milford Wigle learned—as had thousands of pioneers before them—that coming down the western slope of the Cascades could be a treacherous undertaking. They had been granted free passage over the Willamette Valley and Cascade Mountain toll road, after which came the precarious trip down Seven Mile Mountain and the Santiam road to Sweet Home.

If they had it to do over again, Huss and Wigle might have winched their car down the 50 percent grade as pioneer wagon masters had done decades before. Instead, they set the brakes on the road-weary runabout, and with Huss at the tiller and Wigle sliding along behind, they came screeching down the rough, precipitous canyon trail. More than once the vehicle almost got out of control—but with a mite of skill and a mountain of luck, the indomitable duo and Old Scout survived the suicidal descent. (In Old Steady, Megargel and Stanchfield had a wilder ride, as their car struck a rock and threw both of them into the underbrush before it came to a stop on the edge of a cliff!) From then on, though, the final few miles were a breeze.

On June 21 at Oregon City a delegation from the Portland Automobile Club met the front-runner. As the gala procession entered Portland, thousands of happy people (awaiting the opening of the Lewis and Clark Exposition) roared their approval. Huss and Wigle had sliced it pretty thin! They delivered official greetings from Melville E. Stone, manager of the Associated Press in New York, to President H. W. Goode of the centennial celebration just 62 minutes before the gates were thrown open to the jubilant throng. The message read in part:

The century which has just passed was chiefly notable as the century which developed inter-communication. It was the century out of which came the ocean steamship, the railway, rotary and perfecting printing presses, stereotyping, news gathering associations and the newspapers.

But nothing could better illustrate the progress of 100 years than a comparison of this new expedition by a twentieth century motor car from the Atlantic seaboard to the land "where rolls the Oregon," with that other expedition of Lewis and Clark, which meant so much for our common country and the world's civilization.

The cross-country competition was a publicity triumph for the Olds Motor Works, even though it was a few days later before Old Steady made a somewhat belated entrance at the exposition grounds. As long as one car finished, though, an Oldsmobile had been a sure cinch to win America's first transcontinental "race"—and that's the way the company promotion men wanted it!

SOMEBODY WALKED HOME? One result of endurance runs was to "get the bugs out" of car manu-facture, to toughen them for longer distance driving. (The Smithsonian Institution).

TRIP THROUGH IOWA was particularly bad, especially in bottom lands along Skunk River where heavy rains created a giant bog. Yet teams got through—with shovels, winches and muscle. In Omaha, Neb. (left) the two teams made extra preparations for assault on relatively uncharted roads of West. They separated soon after and were never together for rest of trek. Escort vehicle here was White steamer.

EVERYWHERE CARS STOPPED (opposite top) they drew bevvies of youngsters, mostly boys to grow up in new automotive age. Appearances of Old Scout and Old Steady were occasions of long-remembered excitement in small communities. In Laramie, Wyo. (opposite bottom), reception committee greeted Old Scout. Weather was not so hospitable however as teams encountered hail and May snowstorm before they left state. (All photos this page Oldsmobile Div. General Motors Corp.).

DWIGHT HUSS, driver of Old Scout (top row left) took momentary breather before plunging on through sagebrush. Stubborn desert plant which grew right in middle of roads battered front and bottom of the two cars and made driving difficult (Minnesota Historical Society) . . . In Pauline, Ore. (center) Old Scout attracted usual throng of curious spectators. Not long afterwards Huss and Wigle made near-disastrous run down Seven Mile Mountain on western side of Cascades. (Right) Old Steady was hung up in tire-ripping lava beds of Idaho. Smooth-surface pneumatics were particularly vulnerable to sharp, jagged rocks. (Photos Oldsmobile Div. General Motors Corp.).

HUSS AND WIGLE (opposite) were greeted by Pres. H. W. Goode of Lewis and Clark Exposition in Portland, Ore. just 62 minutes before gala event was declared open. Old Steady arrived several days later. (Oldsmobile Div. General Motors Corp.).

END OF THE ROAD! At Glacier Park Lodge in Montana, Dr. James D. Park introduced his 1909 Locomobile to 4 unsmiling Indian passengers. (Great Northern Railway).

THE GLIDDEN TOURS
... One last grand gasp

Charles Jasper Glidden—ex-telegraph messenger, intrepid balloonist and telephone pioneer—believed more in fostering the reliability of automobiles rather than their speed. That's the main reason he has found a special niche in automotive annals as instigator and promoter of the historic tours which bore his name. Glidden had participated in the group trip from New York City to the Louisiana Purchase Exposition in St. Louis in 1904; it had convinced him that such tours were exciting experiences for motorists, though he felt they should be better organized and have a greater purpose than being a mere mechanized fun-fest.

The fledgling American Automobile Association agreed to the sponsorship of a yearly long-distance reliability run. Only stock cars would be allowed to participate; speed was to be a secondary objective, though time limits were established; penalties would be imposed for tardiness, breakdowns and automotive deficiencies. A giant silver trophy, known as the Glidden Cup, was created to honor the best performance.

The first Glidden Tour took place in 1905. It was routed from New York City to Bretton Woods, New Hampshire, and return, a total of 870 miles. Percy Pierce in a Pierce-Arrow won the prize, but more important, the excursion captured the fancy of owners and hopeful owners everywhere, and the annual Glidden cavalcade quickly became the highlight of the motoring year. From 1905 through 1911 the touring event attracted numerous entries, including women drivers and passengers. However, in 1911, the 1,396-mile junket from New York City to Jacksonville, Florida, was so bedeviled with miserable weather and worse roads (one driver was killed near Tipton, Georgia) that the good reputation of the Glidden Tours was seriously tarnished. Then, too, the auto was no longer a novelty to a great many American people, so one of the original attention-getting factors of the treks through the hinterlands—to introduce motoring to the uninitiated—was also lost. As a result, the participant interest was so feeble in 1912 that the AAA decided to cancel the event. Not so Charles Glidden! All by himself he made a 1,272-mile run from Detroit to New

EVEN IN WIDE OPEN SPACES it was somehow possible to slither off road. Such accidents marked first two days of 1913 Glidden Tour, last of famous auto excursions. (Great Northern Railway).

Orleans just to keep the string alive. His persistence resulted in one last grand gasp for the historic tours the following year.

In 1913 Glidden found an unlikely ally in Louis W. Hill, Sr., chairman of the board of the Great Northern Railway. Hill didn't consider the autos of the day as competitive to his transcontinental line, so when the idea of a car tour from Minneapolis to Glacier Park in Montana was proposed, the railroad magnate magnanimously offered to do what he could to make the junket a huge success. And he did plenty! (Mr. Hill, to keep the record straight, also recognized that the venture would be good publicity for the Great Northern and for the newly established park served by his road.)

First of all, he arranged for a special "hotel" train to provide food, lodging, liquid refreshments and repair facilities along the entire route. Basic components of the train included six sleepers, two diners and an observation car. A garage car was equipped to service the autos along the way. And for promotional purposes, Hill wisely included a newspaper car, complete with darkroom, photoengraving plant, linotype, a small cylinder press and mailing facilities. Newsmen on the assignment had a journalistic picnic publishing a four-page daily called the **Glacier Park Blazer.**

Meanwhile, with the Minnesota auto clubs generating most of the enthusiasm, plans were made for the tour itself. Rules were relaxed to lure more entries. The itinerary was plotted so that the train with all the goodies would always be near at hand. The pilot car—a Mitchell—was loaded with confetti to mark the route for the two dozen official participant cars. Mechanics had to work around the clock to restore two Metz autos which had arrived in Minneapolis by rail from Waltham, Massachusetts; somewhere enroute, thieves had removed tires, headlights, tanks and whatever else they could unbolt and tote away.

Finally, in the early morning of July 11, the merry travelers were ready for their prairie safari—but a soggy safari it promised to be! The rains came, and when the pilot car departed at 7 a.m., Dr. Charles E. Dutton of Minneapolis—the referee—suggested that decoy ducks might prove to be better road markers than wet confetti. At 8:30 the pacemaker car—also a Mitchell—splashed away from the starting post, followed by American Automobile Association officials in a Winton, and the press corps in a Paige. Immediately afterward, a Packard driven by President Hill of the Great Northern started out as the leading entry. (Once he got the vehicle underway, Hill slipped out of the car and returned to his dry office in St. Paul.) At 30-second intervals, the other autos rolled out, with designated speeds—ranging from 16 to 20 miles per hour—assigned according to size and price of the model.

Unlike the earlier Glidden cavalcades, this one featured a majority of privately-owned or dealer-sponsored cars. By this time manufacturers had wisened up sufficiently so that they hesitated to enter their products in a competition where they could come in last as well as first; they preferred to stage their own "tests" which they'd be sure to win or at

least control. Nonetheless, the Metz Auto Company entered three Model 22 roadsters (including the burglarized pair); the Krit Motor Car Company of Detroit signed up a trio of runabouts; and two Hupmobiles bore the banner of Rudolph W. Munzer & Sons, Minneapolis distributors. The starting list also included such names as Marmon, Premier, Stutz, Little, Moon, Chalmers and Locomobile, but along the route individual motorists joined the caravan for all or part of a day's run, so that the average number in the gala procession exceeded 150 cars.

The first leg of the journey—140 miles from Minneapolis to Alexandria, Minnesota—was no joyous Sunday cruise. The steady downpour turned the generally poor roads to consistently miserable ones. Nearly every entry was in the ditch at one time or another. Five miles east of Osakis, the pilot car slithered off the road, smashed through a fence and settled oozingly in the mud. A farmer with his horses finally got it back into action. The referee's pacemaker Mitchell also got stuck, and the official tour flag was transferred to a Stutz driven by Frederick C. Legg. Needless to say, the hotel train was much appreciated when the motorists sloshed into Alexandria that night.

The second day wasn't much better. The rainstorm continued until mid-afternoon, and the mishaps were frequent. Again it was the pilot car which got into the most trouble. Some 19 miles east of Fergus Falls it came to rest precariously in four feet of water. This time it took another team and eight men to get it back on the road. To complicate matters, all the oil ran out of the crankcase, and unknowingly the driver headed down the sodden highway only to have a piston freeze up. The confetti was promptly shifted to the press car. When the downpour subsided, conditions improved, and all entries—including the pilot Mitchell—made it to Fargo, North Dakota. The next day was Sunday, and everybody took advantage of it to dry out and recuperate.

On Monday the trip resumed again, up the Minnesota side of the Red River to Crookston, then west to Grand Forks and finally Devils Lake. The gumbo roads of the river valley clung to the autos like feathers to a tar-baby; many radiators over-heated, but most of the vehicles kept out of the ditches. Once on the more firm footing of the drier prairies, the participants perked up, malfunctions were less frequent and the pace accelerated. Under clear skies, citizens of the tiny towns along the route turned out to greet the sojourners with banners, brass bands and even a few pistol shots. The arrival in Devils Lake was a flag-waving, horn-tooting event!

It was not a particularly happy occasion for one of the newspapermen with the entourage, however.

Some practical joker had advertised in the **Devils Lake Daily Journal** that reporter Eddie Westlake of the **Chicago Post** was a cat-lover and would pay a dollar apiece for all felines brought to him at the tour train. This sounded like easy money to a gang of young entrepreneurs who rounded up all the stray tabbies in town and were waiting for the unappreciative Westlake when the press car pulled up.

From Devils Lake the caravan proceeded quite uneventfully to Minot, but the next day's stint—across the hills and bench lands to Williston—was something else again. At one point the pacemaker lost the confetti trail and led a dozen entrants on a meandering follow-the-leader course through the rugged countryside. Blowouts and punctures were common; so were broken springs and radiators. A few headlamps were lost, and the Stutz was sidelined when a rock ripped a hole in its crankcase. The ensuing run to Glasgow, Montana, wasn't much better. A burned-out clutch eliminated the Marmon; the pacemaker Mitchell hit a culvert and suffered a broken steering knuckle. Dust became a problem, and so did the sun. Some men quit shaving because of sunburn; others smeared on cold cream or wore bandannas over their faces like holdup men.

At Poplar, Montana, the motorists were "raided" by a band of mounted Blackfoot Indians, led by a horseman who seemed oddly familiar. It was, as it turned out, President Louis Hill of the Great Northern, who had a jolly good time participating in the "attack." Later he joined the caravan for the remainder of the trip.

The seventh day of driving took the tourists from Glasgow to Havre where they were guests at a civic celebration and banquet. Then, on the eighth day (ninth counting the Sunday off in Fargo), they arrived —weary but happy—at the Glacier Park Hotel. Seven autos completed the journey with perfect scores, having made it to each control point along the way in the allotted time. Two of them, however, just barely qualified on the final lap. Dr. James D. Park roared across the finish line with just seconds to spare after giving his passengers a wild circus ride in his 1909 Locomobile. Right along with him was Clarence Munzer who limped in with two flat tires on his Hupmobile; he promptly collapsed and had to be revived by the cheering spectators. The other Hupmobile and all three Metz roadsters escaped penalties. So, too, did one of the K.R.I.T. runabouts piloted by Frank A. Witt of Detroit and his vivacious young wife.

The coveted Glidden Cup went to the Metz team, and congratulatory toasts were drunk far into the night. The celebrants didn't know it at the time, but they were also toasting the end of the "King of Tours."

GLIDDEN TOURS tested the mettle of men and the metal of machines. (American Automobile Association).

THE PRESS CAR (top) contained darkroom facilities for photographers as well as engraving plant which allowed pictorial evidence of journey for newspapers along route and provided illustrations for "Glacier Park Blazer" . . . Above, reporter Eddie Westlake of Chicago "Post" was victim of practical jokester in Devils Lake, N.D. An advertisement in local paper said he'd pay a dollar apiece for cats. Enterprising youngsters greeted him with motley collection of strays . . . Press car also included complete print shop producing daily newspaper (below), "Glacier Park Blazer" which provided detailed record of historic tour. (Photos Great Northern Railway).

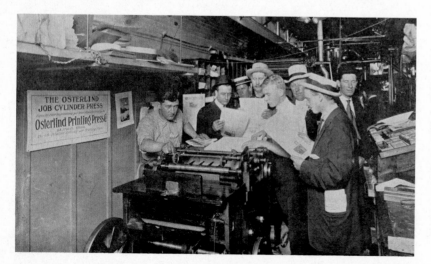

WHEREVER TRAIN OR TOUR CARS visited in Minnesota, North Dakota and Montana, great crowds gathered to w i t n e s s excitement. Many local motorists then joined caravan and accompanied it for part of trip. (Great Northern Railway).

BOTH PACEMAKER AND PILOT CARS (right) were Mitchells. They were spick-and-span when leaving Minneapolis morning of July 11 but before end of first day each was mired in mud. Referee suggested decoy ducks might make better road markers than soggy confetti. (Great Northern Railway).

GARAGE CAR (2 photos left) was welcome unit of tour train. It carried complete facilities to keep automobiles in operation. Welding equipment was especially busy in rugged country west of Red River Valley. On narrow, muddy road one car could hold up entire cavalcade (above center) but there was plenty of help for mired vehicle. As Glidden Tours went, final event lacked rigors of several earlier junkets. (Photos Great Northern Railway).

BROKEN SPRING (above right) was welded at scene of trouble, all part of service provided by Louis W. Hill Sr., board chairman Great Northern Railway. Earlier Glidden Tours were not so well favored. Drivers and their guests were wined and dined on hotel train (right), feature of final Glidden Tour which separated it from all others. Participants traveled along railroad track in style, knowing hot bath, good meal and soft bed were awaiting them at end of day's run. (Photos Great Northern Railway).

Ruts they called ROADS

Judging from the condition of American roads in the pioneer days of motoring, Oliver Evans may well have had a brilliant idea with his **Oruktor Amphibolos** in 1805. A vehicle which would travel as successfully in water as on land was probably better adapted to the so-called highways of the early 1900s than conventional autos of the period.

When the Duryea brothers displayed their tiny car for the first time in 1893, the United States already had about two million miles of rural roads. Unfortunately, most of them were dirt—narrow, winding, shoulder-less and ill-tended. When it rained, they were generally impassable; when it didn't, they were dusty and deeply rutted, hardly fit for a cattle drive let alone automobile travel.

In the beginning, motorists swung little weight with the road-building authorities. As a matter of fact, the earliest "good roads" movements were fostered, not by auto fanciers, but by the bicyclists of the 1890s. The League of American Wheelmen for instance, was a national organization which, in the final two decades of the 19th century, was highly influential in advocating improved inter-city highways. Cycling was more than just a fad at the time. In 1874 H. J. Lawson invented the first so-called safety bicycle, a chain-driven device with two medium-sized wheels of equal diameter. Up until that time the dangerous high-wheelers were limited to the intrepid and the foolhardy. Only long-legged men could achieve any speed, and the ladies, of course, would have little to do with such an unfeminine contraption.

But with the advent of the safety bike and the introduction of pneumatic tires by John Boyd Dunlop in 1888, it became possible for almost anybody to own and manipulate a bicycle. Manufacturers (many of whom—like Col. Albert A. Pope, Thomas B. Jeffery

(Opposite page) AMERICAN AUTOMOBILE ASSOCIATION, through its sponsorship of reliability runs and other tours, emphasized national need for better roads—mostly by getting stuck in them. (American Automobile Association) . . . Whacking out stumps (above) was all in day's work for pioneer motorists who wisely carried axes, shovels, winching equipment on inter-city trips. This 1910 Oldsmobile was hung up in Kentucky. (General Motors Corporation).

and the White brothers—later turned from bikes to motor cars) produced millions of the two-wheelers. The more owners there were, the more they wanted to pedal farther and farther out into the country. The gouged-up farm trails and the rough, untended routes taken by wagon freighters and stage coaches simply weren't conducive to comfortable cycling. So the Wheelmen (from whom evolved the American Road Builders Association) began to put ever-increasing pressure on Congress to do something about the national byways.

The effort was sufficiently successful to achieve the establishment in 1893 of the U. S. Office of Road Inquiry under the Department of Agriculture. The law, signed by President Benjamin Harrison, read in part:

> "To enable the Secretary of Agriculture to make inquiries in regard to the system of road management throughout the United States, to make investigations in regard to the best methods of road-making, and to enable him to assist the agricultural colleges and experiment stations in disseminating information on this subject, ten thousand dollars."

Roads, of course, had always been of great importance to the young nation. Their development, however, was slow and disorganized. Indian pathways and the trails of deer, elk and bison were the primitive beginnings. The historical Connecticut Path—from Boston to Hartford—became the first of the Boston Post Roads. Whenever possible, colonists used water travel—by steam, lake or canal—but sooner or later the need for over-land routes became necessary. The corduroy technique of surfacing trails with half-logs—split longitudinally—was tried and found axle-breaking and spine-smashing.

The new states, heavily in debt from the Revolutionary War, had no money for road improvement, so the turnpike system was adopted. Private companies were authorized to build and operate roads along the main routes of travel. A pike or pole guarded each entrance to these toll highways, and when a traveler paid the proper fee, the pike was turned to permit him to pass—thus the term "turnpike." For almost a half century such pay-as-you-go roads were common; New York State alone had 400 of them at one period in the early 1800s. Gravel and crushed stone were sometimes used as surfacing materials, but the roads were mostly dirt, or, more often than not, mud. Travel in winter and early spring was virtually impossible; it was not too good at other times either. Occasionally a turnpike company would erect a bridge, but usually streams had to be forded—which also meant that roads had to meander considerably to lead to the shallow spots in rivers and creeks.

Through most of the 19th century, road building and maintenance became the function of county and local governments. Money for such work was scarce; the demand for transportation facilities was not so great that politicians had to fear for lack of action. Added to that, the engineering technology (to which the Romans especially had contributed so much centuries before) had lagged woefully. Road care in many instances was accomplished by farmers working out their tax bills. With crude scoops and drags pulled by horses, they tried to keep chuckholes filled and fallen trees removed. There was little thought to other more sophisticated considerations.

As early as 1796 the Philadelphia-Lancaster Turnpike had been constructed with a 24-foot wide surface of crushed stone along its entire 62-mile length. But it was an exception. The cost of $7,500 per mile was generally prohibitive during the many years when there were no specific sources of revenues for such projects. (Oregon levied the first gas tax in 1919, for instance.) The Lancaster Turnpike was a pioneer example of macadamizing, a method of road-building using crushed rock on a prepared bed. The technique was named for John Loudon MacAdam, whose experiments in Scotland were a major contribution to early-day civil engineering.

Course rock roads were no better for cyclists, though, than muddy quagmires, so when the Wheelmen began to assert their strength, new surfacing techniques came under consideration. Four miles of brick pavement were laid on the Wooster Pike near Cleveland, Ohio, in 1893, the first such hard-topped rural road in the U. S. Almost concurrently in Bellefontaine, Ohio, the first concrete paving was poured on Court Avenue. Since the Duryea horseless carriage shared the same birth year, it can readily be argued that 1893 marked the beginning of a new era of transportation in America.

While the automobile did not replace the bicycle as it did the horse, it certainly shoved the manually-pedalled vehicle aside. Bikes became the transport for youngsters, Western Union messengers, certain college students and health enthusiasts. Even the U. S. Army dropped its plans for a bicycle corps, as it speculated laggardly on the possible use of motorized equipment. But the Wheelmen had done the earliest auto operators a great service by calling national attention to the miserable shape of the country's roads. After that, the responsibility for keeping the spotlight on highway needs shifted to the rapidly growing car caste.

Realiability runs, transcontinental races and group tours emphasized just how bad the situation really was, especially west of the Mississippi River. Lack of county-by-county and state-by-state coordination created some frustrating conditions. A motorist had no guarantee that a road in one governmental jurisdiction would continue once he reached the border. There was absolutely no uniformity of construction; engineering niceties were negligible; right-angle turns were commonplace, and it was not unusual for a two-lane road to split around a tree or giant boulder. Travel in the mountains required sheer bravery, a block-and-tackle and a litany of deliverance. Still, the concept of a unified road-construction program was slow in coming.

A Federal Good Roads bill—the first of its kind—died in a congressional committee in 1903. Roads were a prerogative of states' rights, but the states weren't doing much about them. As early as 1891, though, New Jersey had initiated a state-aid program to the counties, and by the turn of the century six other commonwealths had followed suit. The effort, however, was feeble and under-financed. Office-holders used road jobs for patronage and pay-off; graft— petty and monstrous—was often involved. No wonder Carl G. Fisher, a founder of the Prest-O-Lite Company and the Indianapolis Speedway, wrote in 1912: ". . . . the highways of America are built chiefly of politics, whereas the proper material is crushed rock or concrete." That year Congress appropriated $500,000 to assist the states in the improvement of postal routes. It was a meager beginning.

Two years later—with more than three and a half million motor vehicles on U. S. roads (or up to their hubcaps in them)—the nation had less than $15,000 miles of hard-topped highways. Greater action was imperative, and it came finally in 1916. On July 11 that year President Woodrow Wilson signed the Federal Aid Road Act (the Tice Law), the first legislation drafted to establish a nation-wide system of interstate highways. The act provided for the construction or rural public roads and defined them as "any public road over which the United States mails now or may hereafter be transported." It called for federal matching funds up to 50 percent for the highway construction, but, more important, it insisted upon the creation of state highway departments to administer building programs—or no federal money would be forthcoming. By 1919 all 48 states were in

the road business, and the stage was set for the development of a true network of roads rather than willy-nilly byways.

The U. S. Bureau of Public Roads was created immediately following World War I. In 1921 a second Federal Highway Act more clearly defined the aid program to develop a gigantic national road system. The Kahn-Wadsworth bill made possible the distribution of more than 25,000 surplus army trucks and other equipment to the state highway departments for road-building purposes.

Meanwhile, the undaunted motorists persisted and seemingly thrived under deplorable conditions. They took their lumps and bounced back for more. The spirit of adventure prevailed for many years and helped alleviate the difficulties of pioneer motoring. Then, too, a generation of hardy individuals—long used to the discomforts and drudgeries of horse-powered transport—found it easy to adjust to the physical demands and the mental anguish of a trip by car. Mud, dust, jagged rocks and bridge-less streams were readily accepted as "par for the course," and it was probably this acceptance of things as they were" which made it possible for the early-day autoists to survive the rigors of the road and actually rise above them!

WITH ITS WIRE WHEELS and low, sporty look, this Metz friction-drive roadster was talk of Ramona, Okla., circa 1914. (Div. of Manuscripts, University of Oklahoma Library).

PICTURES DO NOT LIE? . . . but too many of the same type can create erroneous impression. Certainly mud was curse of pioneer motorists but photographers tended to concentrate lenses on mired cars rather than on those purring along smoothly on dry roadbeds. Weighted evidence could indicate early day autoists never had any fun but this was not the case. (Photos both pages General Motors Corp.; American Automobile Assn.; The Smithsonian Institution; U. S. Bureau of Public Roads).

THIS MUD HOLE (opposite) in road near Ironton, Ohio, served one purpose. It was typical enough so Delco selected it to field-test certain automotive equipment in 1921. (Delco Products Div. General Motors Corp).

E-M-F STOOD FOR EVERETT-METZGER-FLANDERS, but in situations like these (above and below), it might well have been Ever-Mud-Fast. Glidden Tour members who followed pathfinder car were in for more of same. (Photos American Automobile Association).

PARTICULARLY IN WEST roads were often "where you made them." Mostly small streams had to be forded, so a good driver must zigzag his way between rocks and driftwood. Dodge touring car (above) demonstrated its rugged constitution. (Chrysler Corporation) . . . Rail fences came in handy (below left) to provide pry bars for marooned motorists. (The Smithsonian Institution) . . . In Osborne Co., Kansas (below right), mud-bound drivers had to grin and bear it until somebody went for horse. (The Kansas State Historical Society).

BRIDGES WERE RARE in pioneer days of motoring so roads meandered to shallow places in rivers and creeks. Scoop-nosed Franklin (top left) and Ford Model T (above) were photographed at typical fording sites. (American Automobile Assn.). White's Ferry (left) on Potomac River emphasized difficulties of getting auto from one side of major stream to other. Carl H. Claudy took this picture about 1905. (The Smithsonian Institution).

EVEN WHEN BRIDGES WERE
BUILT they were not always trust-
w o r t h y. Designed primarily for
horse and buggy, many could not
hold up added weight of autos and
trucks, especially if spans were
weakened by swollen streams. (King
County, Wash. Engineer).

89

CHAINS WERE MANDATORY for any kind of wet weather driving (above). Even then it was possible to sink axle-deep into muck. Pioneer motorists were a hardy lot however, seemingly able to accept discomforts and hardships. (General Motors Corporation) . . . Desert driving required special tires to keep from sinking in fine sand. Low-slung autos had particular trouble (below) where roads hid in sage brush, itself formidable obstacle. (American Automobile Assn.).

AUTOMOBILE CLUB OF MINNE-
APOLIS took matters into own hands
(two views above) by actually participating in maintenance of public
roads . . . as did other motoring
organizations in pre-World War I
era before state highway departments generally assumed responsibility. (Photos Minnesota Historical
Society).

ONE-MILE STRETCH of concrete
road (right) in Wayne County, Mich.
was welcomed as answer to America's highway problems in 1909. By
modern standards it was narrow
and dangerous—but it was a start.
(Portland Cement Assn.).

COVERED BRIDGES had charm all their own. They were also a welcome haven to automobilists (as pioneer drivers were sometimes called) caught by unexpected showers in open-air vehicles. (Ford Motor Company Archives).

WHEN WEATHER WAS GOOD, dirt and gravel roads could be rustic and appealing like El Camino Real (left) near Atherton, Calif. (Worden Collection, Wells Fargo Bank History Room).

ROAD BUILDING WAS SLOW (above) and relatively unscientific when horses and local farmers were depended upon to get job done. After World War I surplus army trucks were assigned the task. (Photos Michigan State Highway Department). One-lane concrete farm to market roads (right) were experimented with during early 1920s. Loaded trucks or farm wagons used concrete land enroute to market. Empty vehicles used unpaved shoulder on way home. (Portland Cement Assn.).

1908 PREMIER (below) passed toll gate in state of New York in this vintage photo. Pay-as-you-go roads were outgrowth of demand for better highways at time when states and counties did not have finances for purpose. (American Automobile Assn.)

THE MODEL T HAULED EVERYTHING! No doubt some wag chided this owner about a goat's liking for tin cans. (Ford Motor Company Archives).

SYMBOL OF AN ERA...
the Triumphant T

"I will build a motor car for the great multitudes. It will be large enough for the family but small enough for individuals to run and care for. It will be constructed of the best materials, by the best men to be hired, after the simplest designs that modern engineering can devise. But it will be so low in price that no man making a good salary will be unable to own one—and enjoy with his family the blessing of hours of pleasure in God's great and open spaces."

Henry Ford said that. He also translated his words into reality in the form of a gawky, angular mechanical Ichabod Crane—a piece of unesthetic machinery which changed not only the automobile industry but America as well. No high sounding promotion name accompanied the introduction of Ford's "car for the multitudes." When it came off the production line, it was known simply as the Model T; before it eight other letters of the alphabet were used to designate production models; other letters had been assigned to experimental units and cars which never quite made it. In the chronology of the company, the T just happened to come up like a jackpot symbol on a giant industrial slot machine. Somehow it seemed to be the perfect semantic marriage; the Model T entered the language and lives of the American people as no other automobile has, before or since.

Not even the most sophisticated computer will ever be able to recount how many individuals have been affected by Ford's automotive phenomenon. One could start, of course, with a basic figure of 15,000,000, because that's how many Model Ts were made from 1908 to 1927. The families of the original owners had to be included as direct beneficiaries of the ubiquitous Tin Lizzie. But that was just the beginning!

The Model T, unlike the cat, REALLY had more than a single life. It was the world's greatest hand-me-down car. Once it finished its original task, it went on to other assignments, often passing from owner to owner until literally hundreds of people were involved in its life history. It certainly was not the world's best car. Or the prettiest. Or the most powerful. But when it came to versatility, the T was a veritable chameleon. With flanged wheels

EVEN UBIQUITOUS T occasionally succumbed to mud. Yet it was relatively light, uncomplicated—and it was easy to hitch a team to its front axle. (Ford Motor Company Archives).

it operated on railroad tracks; with skis and cater-pillar-type treads it scooted across snow-covered prairies; with rear-end jacked up, it operated buzz saws, grinding mills, cement mixers and hay stack-ers. There were Model T fire engines, construction jitneys, school buses, ambulances, paddy wagons and delivery trucks of every description. Itinerant scissors-grinders mounted their equipment on the back of a Tin Lizzie and made their door-to-door calls. So did fish and fruit peddlers. With a shortened wheel base and a roller in the back, a bucking Model T of clowns or local characters was a parade favorite from one end of the nation to the other. It was truly an American institution—both loved and scorned, praised and ridiculed. In many respects, it had many of the characteristics of its creator, as if it were possible for some hereditary factors to pass from flesh and blood to steel, wood and leather.

It is doubtful whether Henry Ford himself could have anticipated the phenomenal success of his low-priced car. Against the counsel of friends and ad-visers, he plunged ahead on his revolutionary phil-osophy. Automobiles did not have to be the ex-clusive property of the rich. Keep them simple, standard and cheap, and all America could be on wheels. That he was right is now 20/20 historical hind-sight. His adaptations of the principles of mass-production need little re-telling. His concept of stand-ardization has been epitomized in his all-too-serious quip: "Any customer can have a car painted any colour he wants . . . so long as it is black." He was 45 years old when the Model T was born—old enough to know better, some of his associates thought—but Henry Ford, like his famous flivver, was stubborn and unchanging.

Production of the Model T ranged from 16 cars a week in 1909 to 8,000 a day in 1926. During the 19-year span, an average of more than 2,200 Model Ts came off the line every day—approximately 1.6 Lizzies per minute around the clock from the fall of 1908 to the spring of 1927. The latter year, of course, marked the end of the road for the change-less "box of tin" which had been reproduced by the millions like a gingerbread car stamped out by a giant cookie-cutter. Dwindling sales and the grow-ing success of competitors — especially General Motors — finally convinced Ford that he had over-played his hand. The people DID want color. In the period of prosperity which preceded the Great Depression, they were willing to pay a hundred dollars or more for style. The planetary transmis-sion, the mechanical brake and the four-cylinder engine were no longer adequate to satisfy a buying public now grown attuned to the automobile.

So—just as he did on January 5, 1914, with the announcement of his revolutionary $5 minimum wage—Henry Ford again made the grand gesture. He shut down his plants, re-tooled completely and on December 2, 1927, rolled out the first Model A. Only Charles A. Lindbergh's flight across the Atlantic earlier that year attracted as much national interest.

Just because production stopped, however, the Model T did not die with the birth of its successor. There were still millions of them operating in the United States and throughout the world, and they continued to be active in great numbers at least until World War II. Three generations of American men — grandfathers, fathers and sons — knew the Model T intimately. Grandmothers, mothers and daughters, too, could recount endless experiences in the jaunty little jalopy which nobody loved but the people.

Only mothers-in-law, politicians and traveling sales-men sparked the humorists of the period to a degree comparable to the funnybone-tickling T. Anyone who didn't know the latest Ford joke was a social pariah. There were stories about little old ladies from lots of places who sent in a year's supply of tomato cans to Detroit—and got back a Model T, and three cans left over. The wags said that Henry was going to paint all his flivvers yellow so they could be sold in bunches like bananas. Or that he was going to have to paint them all red to obey the law about tin cans carrying gasoline. Or that he was going to deliver all cars with a can-opener and no doors; each new owner could cut his own to suit himself. Or the mechanic who said: "My advice to you, sir, is to keep the oil and change the car."

Though the connotations were generally bad, the publicity was good, and people kept buying Fords almost as fast as the company could make them. And that was pretty fast, according to the gagsters. One assembly line worker dropped his wrench, they said, and before he could pick it up, 16 cars were on the highways without brakes. A minister was supposed to have ranted from his pulpit that the Ford car was carrying more people to damnation than anything yet conceived by man. "Don't worry," retorted a member of the congregation, "the Model T has never gone anywhere it can't get back from, so I reckon all those folks in hell will be making the return trip any day now."

Just as the Model T had kindled the American sense of humor, it also had a similar effect on native inventiveness. Viewed in retrospect, Henry Ford could well have taken a warning from the multi-million dollar industry which grew up to fill the gnawing desire of owners who wanted to make the standardized T look and act like something different than what it was. The F. H. Lawson Company of Cincinnati said it would disguise the Ford by replac-ing the "tin can" hood with a streamlined motor bon-net. The Grigsby Manufacturing Company of Chicago offered to "doll up your Ford for a dollar" with a fancy radiator cap. For less than $100, the Hine-Watt Manufacturing Company, also of Chicago, would pro-vide a "Snappy-Sport" body easily mounted on a Model T chassis; it came in several colors, including Stutz Red and Brewster Green. Capitalizing on Model T shortcomings, opportunistic firms came out with special brake attachments, shock absorbers, mufflers and scores of other gadgets and gimcracks—some practical, some ridiculous. The Model T owner was much like a fishing enthusiast—always being badger-ed into buying something new for his tackle box, whether he needed it or not.

Like Old Dobbin before it, the fabled bucket-o'-bolts finally outlived its usefulness. They say Henry Ford was an inveterate practical joker (he once put wooden croutons in Harvey Firestone's soup), and there are those who insist that the Model T may well have been his impish masterpiece. If so (and no pun intended), his practical joke backfired, and millions of motorists who otherwise may never have been able to afford an auto—got the last laugh.

Henry Ford, of course, always had a few million dollars of Model T profits to console himself.

EVEN THE TIN LIZZIE could get stuck in the mud as evidenced by this photo (above) taken near Gwinner, N.D. It was light enough, however, to make rescue operations relatively easy. (Melroe Company) . . . After it served its original purpose the Model T still had a future (below). As a stripped-down jitney, it was used on the farm, in construction work and wherever else versatile, economical transportation was needed. (U.S. Dept. of Agriculture).

MODEL T WAS RIDICULED (above and right) and maligned yet 15 million of them were made, sold and enjoyed. (Photos Ford Motor Company) . . . There were times when motoring was no laughing matter but Ford jokes were seeming endless. Wags asked: "What time is it when one Ford follows another?" Reply: "Tin after tin!" (The Smithsonian Institution).

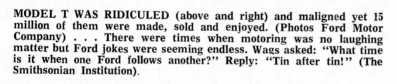

THERE WAS CONTINUING EFFORT to make T something other than what it was. Custom bodies were designed to disguise angular lines, special paint jobs to vary Ford black. Conversion above was made in London, Eng. (Harrah's Automobile Collection).

FAMOUS PEOPLE AND FAMOUS AUTO—Thomas A. Edison (above), Sir Harry Lauder, humorous Scot (below). Yet the T was, as Henry Ford intended it, a "car for the masses". (Top, Harrah's Automobile Collection; bottom, The Free Library of Philadelphia).

WITH FLANGED WHEELS the versatile T became a railroad runabout, ideal for track inspections and executive tours. Closed model saw service on Detroit, Toledo & Ironton Railroad. (Ford Motor Company, top — The Smithsonian Institution, right).

101

OWNER'S IMAGINATION (photos left
and below) was only factor limiting service of Model T. Its commercial uses were
endless and it was popular courting car.
(Photos top to bottom, Mr. and Mrs.
Jorgen Bruget; Shell Motor Company;
Ford Motor Company.).

WHEN POWER WASN'T THERE, winch and brawn had to be applied (above). Many Model T drivers achieved better results on steep hills by turning around and backing up. (Denver Public Library Western Collection.).

1912 TOURABOUT (left) was unique model which could be converted from pleasure car into light work vehicle. Top and rear seat were removable. It was short-lived design, one of many Henry Ford experimented with briefly. (Milwaukee Journal.).

SPORTY T ROADSTER (below) became work vehicle when it towed Utility Trailer, reputedly first such commercial device marketed in U.S. (Union Oil Company of Calif.).

ETHYL GASOLINE was first sold in 1923 at this Dayton, Ohio, filling station. (Delco Products Div. General Motors Corp.).

TIRES PATCHED, TANKS FILLED, HORSES SHOD

In the pioneering days, a person who bought a motor car and learned how to operate it had only half the battle won. His biggest challenge was to keep it filled and functioning!

By the standards of history, the automobile flashed onto the scene like a meteor, changing the entire economy and national way-of-life. No one was really ready for it. Long generations of horse-dominated road transportation had created a complex of supporting industries on which the auto had a drastic effect. Harness-makers, livery stable operators, blacksmiths, carriage and wagon manufacturers, wheelwrights, oats and hay producers, hitching post salesmen and horse doctors were threatended with gradual extinction unless they could somehow adapt themselves to the new horseless contraption. A few of them became venomous car-haters, but most began to read the handwriting on the barn wall and tried to adjust accordingly.

The village blacksmith especially found himself in a transitional role. Since he was usually the town fix-it man, he was the logical choice to assume mechanic's duties when an auto broke down. It wasn't long before the smell of forge and cauterized hoof mingled with that of grease and gasoline. The more alert smithies took on auto dealerships and built small sheds apart from their shops in which to store petroleum products. The latter were, in effect, the crude predecessors of the modern service station.

If the pioneer motorist strayed too far from home, he faced the frustrating problem of separating himself from his fuel supply. He had to have a "nose for gasoline," in an era when petrol was somewhat scarce and its location in any given hamlet unpredictable. The touring autoist usually looked first for the blacksmith shop. If not there, the gas might be available at the general store, the pharmacy, the livery stable, the hardware dealer's or the lumber yard. If he found it at a general store, the merchant most likely took a measuring can to a shed behind the store, filled the can from a barrel, walked through the store again and poured the gasoline into the tank through a chamois-lined funnel (the latter was used to catch the water which usually accumulated in the storage drum). No wonder the dealers were interested in a better method of serving a rapidly growing

clientele! In time a two-wheeled hand tank was devised to bring the gas supply directly to the auto.

By 1907 the idea of a business devoted entirely to the servicing of automobiles was being developed. That year in Seattle, Washington, John McLean, a representative of the Standard Oil Company of California, opened what has been claimed to be the first service station in America. It consisted of an old hot-water tank and a hose under a rough wooden canopy. The gas was delivered by gravity. In the same year the Automobile Gasoline Company and the Oriental Oil Company opened stations in St. Louis, Missouri, and Dallas, Texas, respectively. The former —operated by Harry Grenner and Clem Laessig— was credited with the first chain of drive-in filling stations. Within five years Memphis, Tennessee, could boast a 13-pump outlet, complete with a ladies' restroom and a maid who served ice water to customers. The pumps, however, were in the backyard, not on the street—and the super-service was ahead of its time. Curbside pumps began to appear about 1910, though they were forbidden by law in some communities.

Later Bert S. Harrington, Sr., devised a coin-operated, self-service gas pump which apparently had a promising future until the Underwriters Laboratories ruled "that when and where gasoline is dispensed to automobiles, there must be an experienced attendant present to actually dispense the gasoline."

The oil industry was not created by the automobile. It had, in fact, a half-century start on the vehicle which was to give it such a dominant role in the world economy. In 1850 a method of obtaining liquid hydrocarbons from coal and shale was patented by James Young, a Scotsman. This "coal oil" took the pressure off the dwindling numbers of whales which until that time had been a prime source of illuminating oil. Then, on August 27, 1859, an ex-railroad conductor, Edwin L. Drake, made a revolutionary discovery with a 69-foot well at Titusville, Pennsylvania.

"Rock oil" had previously been collected from ground seepage pools and used for medicinal and other limited purposes. With Drake's successful venture on Oil Creek leading the way, petroleum became available in the United States in great volume. It provided kerosene for millions of lamps, paraffin for candles and candy, hoof and harness oils (that horse again!), lubricants for ships and mills, a "miracle" salve called Vaseline, by-products to make such varied items as varnishes, lacquers, oilcloth and patent leather.

One of the waste elements of the distilling process was an explosive, inflammable substance called "gasolene." For a time, it was actually thrown away, being too dangerous to store until someone found a commercial use for it. A small volume was utilized as a raw material in the production of illuminating gas, refrigerants and anesthetics, while the introduction of gas stoves (not the safest household gadgets ever invented) provided a somewhat limited market. Standard Oil Company advertised a "Deodorized Stove Gasoline," a left-over from the distillation of its "water white" and "prime white" kerosenes.

The petroleum industry was apparently destined for success of a sort, but it had its skeptics. In 1886 Prof. J. P. Lesley, the state geologist of Pennsylvania, told a meeting of the American Institute of Mining:

> I take this opportunity to express my opinion in the strongest terms, that the amazing exhibition of oil which has characterized the last twenty, and will probably characterize the next ten or twenty years, is nevertheless not only geologically but historically a temporary and vanishing phenomenon—one which young men will live to see come to its natural end.

It was, with little question, the most unfounded statement of the century. The internal combustion engine was to leave Professor Lesley standing with historical egg on his face. Yet, his gigantic error in judgment was not so far-fetched at the time. Even when the horseless carriage became a reality, there were other myopic prophets like the good professor who predicted that the motor car, too, would be just a short-lived passing fancy. They couldn't have been more wrong!

While kerosene remained the number one product of the petroleum industry, the gasoline which came out of the process was of extremely high quality. After all, the manufacturers wanted as much kerosene and as little waste as possible. Consequently, the gas had few impurities. However, when the demand was reversed starting in 1911, the producers tried to extract as much gasoline as they could out of the crude, and the resulting auto fuel suffered in turn. That spurred new research—for better refining methods and some sort of anti-knock additive. The "cracking" process developed by Dr. William M. Burton in 1913 improved production, but not the firing of the larger kerosene molecules mixed in with the gas. Meanwhile, Thomas Midgley, Jr., Charles Kettering, T. A. Boyd and others associated with them experimented with such substances as iodine and aniline to improve gasoline efficiency. Their results were too expensive and odoriferous, until the action of

THIS PRIMITIVE FILLING STATION, like others of era, was merely adjunct of blacksmith shop next door. In addition to gasoline, smithy advertised plow repairing and bargain on horseshoes. (Standard Oil Company of Indiana).

tetraethyl lead was discovered in 1923. In 1924 General Motors and Standard Oil Company of New Jersey formed the Ethyl Gasoline Corporation to make and sell the new additive.

Just as he had hauled oats for his horse, the wise motorist carried a spare can of gasoline in his car—probably with a potato jammed over the spout. One instruction manual in 1908 said: "If your engine is warm and you run out of gas, you can nearly always get home on kerosene or alcohol or even bad whiskey." For lubrication he twisted the grease cup caps a turn or two every now and then and squirted oil over the moving parts he could see and reach. When crankcase oil leaked out or burned away, he added more; often this oil was thick as molasses so he had to cut it first with a dash of kerosene. No prudent driver ventured forth without a bucket to dip water from roadside ditches to calm an over-wrought radiator.

But all the automobiles were not totally dependent upon the petroleum industry. The electrics, for instance, with power generated by their self-contained batteries, scooted silently about towns and cities. Unfortunately, they were a little like Cinderella's carriage; they had to be back in the garage before their charge was gone, or they sat pumpkin-like until they were towed in for an electrical transfusion.

Steamers, on the other hand, required kerosene, paraffin or some other fuel to heat the water. Operators of the more than 100 different makes of steam cars had their own unique problems. Until the advent of the flash boiler, it took from ten minutes to a half hour to get up the necessary steam. Vital burner parts had to be kept especially clean. Poorly engineered models had leaky tubes and coils. The control valves and guages on the boilers (which seemingly ran short of water when the supply was most available) confused unschooled operators. The open pilot flame under the cars kept steamers out of public garages and off ferry boats, unless the fire was doused.

No matter what the power source, though, all pioneer autos shared a mutual tire problem. Rubber processors made amazing strides in the development of tires and tubes, but the stresses of weight and speed caused an endless string of blowouts. Those, too, were the days of wood stoves, when householders burned scrap lumber or whatever else they could get. Ashes—containing nails, staples and other bits of sharp metal—were then dumped in the streets to fill chuckholes; narrow, hard-rubber carriage tires were unaffected, but thin-faced pneumatic tires on the motor cars of the era were punctured like so many circus balloons. Hand pumps, rubber patches, an assortment of tire irons and (for some operators) a mule-skinner's vocabulary were major requirements for an auto trip of any extended length.

The invention of the demountable rim in 1903 helped the situation somewhat. It was no longer necessary to repair flats at the scene of the misfortune; mounted spares made it possible to make a reasonably quick switch-over—but it was not uncommon for a driver to limp sullenly home on deflated rubber or a bare rim even after using a couple of spares.

Every facet of automobile manufacturing—from front bumpers to tail lights—has a story of its own, with successes and failures, good ideas and bad. The motor car was not born full-bloom; it evolved gradually as inventive individuals in hundreds of allied industries labored to solve problems and improve the appearance, efficiency, safety, durability and over-all performance of America's automobiles.

A simple thing like a gas guage, for instance, had to be conceived, designed, manufactured and perfected. Henry Ford didn't have one for the early Model Ts; he issued a tiny ruler for the motorist to check his gallonage by stopping, lifting the seat and measuring the liquid in the tank. Among the many devices offered to correct that obviously bad situation was a Gaso-phone, a float-rigged bell which rang when the fuel was almost gone.

Ingenuity was a by-word of pioneer autoists. To check how many miles his car traveled per gallon of gasoline, Charles Duryea tied a rag around the left rear tire and rim, filled the tank and told his daughter, Rhea, to start driving. During the test run, he leaned out and counted how many times the rag went around and then multiplied the total by the circumference of the wheel. Later he divided the amount of gas used into the distance traveled.

The early days of motoring were characterized by such unsophisticated devices and techniques. The automobile pioneer—for all the romance and glamour associated with his era—was really a hardy, dust-eating, grease-splattered, skinned knuckle Spartan of the road. With few skilled mechanics to turn to, the average operator had to be inventive and ingenious in his own right. He made on-the-spot repairs with fence wire and roadside junk. He tinkered and fiddled with carburetors and magnetos. He accepted the obvious necessity of getting his clothes muddy and his finger nails dirty. As the song went, "he got out and got under" to keep his mechanical steed in action.

COMPANY EXECUTIVES (above) admiringly ogled the 1-millionth Buick. David Dunbar Buick, who originally built car of the name, was unsuccessful with it and within a year sold Buick Motor Car Company to William C. Durant. (Buick Motor Div. General Motors Corp).

EARLY DAY DENVER GARAGE was long on help and short on working room. Apprentice mechanics learned from journeymen who were themselves a new breed. Some schools began to offer short courses in auto repair. (Denver Public Library Western Collection).

BUILT IN 1912 this drive-in filling station (below) in Columbus, Ohio, marked departure from usual curb pump or mobile gas cart. (The Standard Oil Company of Ohio) . . . The Automobile Gasoline Company of St. Louis, Mo., built its first outlet in 1907 (above). Venture proved successful, others were added and first service station chain was created. (Shell Oil Company).

LADY ATTENDANT operated this curbside pump (above) in Yakima, Wash. in 1918. Portable carts like one at left preceded stationary models, causing many motorists to complain that they couldn't see what they were getting. (American Petroleum Institute).

(Right top to bottom) ARKANSAS CITY, Kansas, station operator was early exponent of "service;" island pumps and uniformed attendants were innovation of this Oklahoma station; vintage airplane stopped for fill-up in Porterville, Calif.; note price of gas here. (Photos top to bottom—The Kansas State Historical Society, Continental Oil Company, Standard Oil Company of Calif.—2).

IN SMALLER TOWNS like Tribune, Kansas, (opposite bottom) blacksmith shop was garage — horses shod, tires patched, carburetor adjusted. (The Kansas State Historical Society).

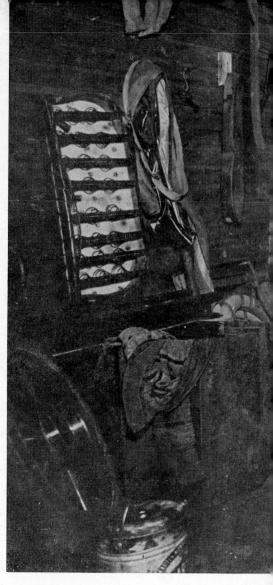

WHEN A. O. SMITH AGREED (top left) to make 10,000 frames for Henry Ford in 4 months, his company was hand operation. 15 years later, in 1921, his Milwaukee plant could produce that many a day on this robot-like line. (A. O. Smith Corp.).

HENRY FORD'S FIRST MOVING ASSEMBLY LINE in 1913 (center and bottom left) revolutionized automobile production. In 2 months system reduced assembly of Model T from 14 hours to 93 minutes. (Photos Ford Motor Company).

TYPICAL PRE-WORLD WAR I GARAGES tended to be rubble-strewn and ill-equipped like Martin Geving's covered blacksmith shop (above) in Nunda, S.D. (Edwin J. Sunde Collection). Somewhat unusual was very orderly garage in Dorrance, Kansas, in 1911 (right) with Maxwell car and Indian motorcycle of same year on floor. (The Kansas State Historical Society).

"THE HORSELESS AGE" MAGAZINE of May, 1896, (left) featured this historic photo of Duryea brothers' factory in Springfield, Mass. During 1895-6, 13 automobiles were built in cramped quarters, first multiple auto production in U.S. (The Smithsonian Institution).

GWINNER, N.D. GARAGE SERVICE CAR (below center) was standard Model T Ford which occasionally had to be rescued itself. On treeless, poleless prairie problem of finding anchor for winch was added complication. (Melroe Company).

BUSINESS END OF TIRE PUMP (bottom) was familiar to all pioneer motorists. Flats often had to be repaired where they occurred. Even if driver had 2 spare tires, it was not unusual to use both and still limp home on bare rim. (American Automobile Assn.).

THIS 1912 GILBERT & BARKER PUMP (above) delivered gallon of gasoline with every hand-operated stroke—photo taken in Massachusetts in 1915. (Mobil Oil Corporation) . . . In Hartford, Conn. (below) curbside service was provided by means of long hose. Development of adequate hoses was problem since gasoline disintegrated rubber of era. (Texaco Archives).

EARLY CARS could never be taken for granted. Roadside tinkering was common, often with plenty of ki-bitzers, as owner of 1906 Bliss (above) found. (John A. Conde Collection). Note front bumper (left), frail beginning of important safety device. (American Automobile Assn.).

ONE PROBLEM OF STEAMERS was continual need for water and burner fuel. This White (above) got fill-up during 1909 Glidden Tour. (Minnesota Historical Society).

ELECTRIC CARS AND TRUCKS were efficient for in-city driving, but drivers had to be alert to get back to garages before batteries ran down. This re-charge station (right) operated in Washington, D.C., circa 1905. (The Smithsonian Institution).

MOTOR TRUCKS began to take over petroleum transport just before World War I. In 1915 hard-tired Kelly-Springfield (below) served stations in San Francisco area. (Shell Oil Company) . . . Ever-present Model T (above) was also used as tank truck. (Standard Oil Company of Calif.)

IN 1915 WRECKER MECHANISM was somewhat complicated. Ernest Holmes Company of Chattanooga, Tenn. (above) was one pioneer in field of auto rescue, motor car replacing horse even more definitely. (American Automobile Association) . . . The pioneer motorist had to be imaginative when it came to repairs. This ingenious fellow (below) borrowed wheel from piece of farm machinery to replace defective one until he could get back to town. (South Dakota Historical Society).

WITH INCREASED SPEEDS came increased dangers, both to motorists and new class of people called pedestrians. In process motorcycle policeman was born. (American Automobile Association).

WHAT'S YOUR
HURRY, BUD?

From the earliest days, automobiles have had a strange affinity for one another. Almost as if manufacturers had adorned them with magnetic bumpers, motor cars began to run into each other, even when there were just two of them in the same town.

At first the major problems occurred when horse met auto. The car-haters over-played the runaways and prophesied all sorts of dire catastrophies for the future. On the other hand, the motor enthusiasts blamed everything on the hay-burners and happily predicted a great new day of personal transportation. Each argument contained an element of truth.

No question about it, the automobile was a boon to mankind—but it was also to prove a killer of people, a destroyer of property and the accomplice of criminals. In 1900 the **New York Tribune** carried the following article:

A young woman was knocked down and fatally injured by an automobile vehicle while crossing Broadway on Christmas afternoon. She was a trained nurse, and therefore presumably intelligent, prudent and active. The vehicle was moving rapidly; just how rapidly is not reported. The engineer in charge of it saw the young woman crossing the street and rang his gong in warning. Apparently, however, he did not abate the speed of the machine nor attempt to steer it out of the way. He considered his responsibility fully discharged by ringing the gong.

Many such stories were to follow in the years ahead. Even in the infancy of motoring—when numbers were few and bad roads precluded great speed —the traffic deaths began to mount. Before the United States entered World War I, auto accidents had killed

THIS UNUSUAL PHOTO of barrel-nosed 1906 air-cooled Franklin was somewhat symbolic. Each year autos were made to go faster and faster—until they finally ran away from themselves. (Harrah's Automobile Collection).

more than 36,000 Americans. By comparison, only 22,424 had lost their lives in the Revolutionary War, the War of 1812, the Mexican War and the Spanish-American War combined. This ridiculous trend—to kill more citizens with cars than with weapons which were **supposed** to destroy people—was to continue to grow worse.

Before the turn of the century, anti-horseless carriage sentiments began to express themselves in restrictive regulations. When Louis Greenough and Harry Adams of Pierre, South Dakota, built a home-made car out of an Elkhart wagon and a two-cylinder Wolverine gas motor in the late 1890s, they envisioned a profitable summer by hauling passengers at county fairs. Not only were they denied permission to carry out their enterprise, but at Mitchell the civic authorities wouldn't even let them bring their gas-mobile inside the city limits.

At the same time, the Boston Board of Aldermen was enacting an amendment to local laws which provided that no person should "in any street use any vehicle, other than a railroad or railway vehicle, or a vehicle of the fire-department, or a vehicle drawn or pushed by an animal, or a vehicle of a construction approved by the Board of Aldermen as not endangering the life or property of others." The mayor vetoed the proposition, but the newly born **Automobile Magazine** took the opportunity to scream bloody murder, not only at the Boston city fathers, but at the citizens of Mount Desert and Bar Harbor in the state of Maine who had drawn up strict rules against the use of motor cars, by summer residents in particular. Earlier yet, Chicago had banned automobiles from public streets, and New York City, more than two decades before, had forced Richard Dudgeon to quit operating his spark-spewing steam road wagon.

Some of the earliest proposals to regulate automobiles were—like the British Red Flag Law—inane and impractical. In Massachusetts an act to require that all cars be equipped with a bell which would ring with each wheel revolution was voted down. Shooting of roman candles to forewarn drivers of approaching horse-drawn vehicles was the silly brainstorm of another lawmaker. The Farmers' Anti-Automobile Society of Pennsylvania demanded that "if a horse is unwilling to pass an automobile, the driver should take the machine apart as rapidly as possible and conceal the parts in the bushes." As late as 1913, the motor law enacted by Montana that year included:

> Every person having control or charge of a motor vehicle shall, whenever upon any public street or highway and approaching any vehicle drawn by horse or horses, mule or mules, or any horse or mule upon which any person is riding, so operate, manage and control such motor vehicle as to exercise every reasonable precaution to prevent the frightening of any such animals and to insure the safety and protection of any person riding or driving the same.

There were laws which required motorists to stop completely while buggies, surreys and freight wagons trundled by. Speed limits of as low as two and three miles-per-hour were imposed by a few cities and towns. In some, night-time driving was forbidden. In 1907 the citizens of Glencoe, Illinois, purposely built humps in the streets to discourage speeding.

Three years earlier a steel cable had been stretched across the road to stop the "devil wagons." Many of these early statutes were more the result of antagonisms against the new mode of transportation rather than an attempt to accomplish any constructive regulation.

In 1899 William Phelps Eno organized the Eno Foundation for Highway Traffic Control. His idea was to compile the common-law rules of the road which had been accepted for generations in Great Britain and apply them to motor vehicles in the United States. A year later he completed a traffic code and submitted it to the City of New York for consideration. It was three years later before his compilation was adopted, but the action marked a giant step toward maturity in the field of traffic regulations. Other cities also accepted the Eno code, and it was revised and reissued several times until World War I.

Meanwhile, other efforts were made. New York City in 1900 issued an engineer's certificate to Harold T. Birnie; it was, in substance, an early example of a driver's license. Various levels of government jumped into the licensing act, resulting in a hodge-podge of regulations covering operation and registration of motor cars. It quickly became apparent that states would have to assume overall jurisdiction, or no one would be able to untangle the mess.

In 1901 Connecticut passed laws regulating the speed and registration of motor vehicles. That same year New York State required "that every vehicle shall have the separate initials of the owner's name placed upon the back thereof in a conspicuous place." That was fine when there were only 954 cars involved, but when registrations increased, the variety of lettering and location of the identifying initials was so great that the state amended the decree and required that assigned registration numbers be shown on plates or leather pads, the latter often made by the local blacksmith or the owner himself.

In 1903 Massachusetts issued the first official state-made license plates, heavy porcelain-enameled white on dark blue tags. Other states followed with numerous variations, including various metal-and-leather combinations, wooden shingles, sheet metal and other do-it-yourself styles. The first state driver's license laws were passed by Rhode Island in 1908 and New Hampshire in 1909.

In the meantime, the jumble of confusing ordinances continued to plague the pioneer motorist. Added to that was a new wrinkle called the "speed trap." In the smaller towns, particularly, over-zealous constables and marshals lay in wait for unsuspecting drivers, timing them by stop-watch of by-guess-and-by-gosh. Some lawmen were authorized to shoot at tires or to stretch chains or wire across the road. Before the motorcycle became an accepted police vehicle, the local gendarmes were somewhat limited in their pursuit of fleeing cars, being either afoot or on bicycle.

There were inequities, of course, and motorists sought ways to defend themselves. One was through organization, and in 1902 the American Automobile Association was formed in Chicago to take up the cudgels for the beleaguered motor car operator. That same year in the same city an ordinance was passed prohibiting the driver of a car to wear **pince-nez** glasses. The A.A.A. proved to be a vigilant watchdog for its members as it fostered realistic regulations and fought against capricious police action, especially the common practice of arresting owners of expensive cars on the premise that such individuals could afford to pay a stiffer fine.

There was no stemming the growing tide of accidents, however. It was a case of simple arithmetic: more cars meant more collisions! With each year, too, the autos were made faster and more powerful. Narrow roads with no shoulders and sharp, unbanked curves simply couldn't accommodate speed runs, and from the beginning — unfortunately! — auto owners have had the insane desire "to see how fast she'll go."

Gradually, as the automobile gave indications of permanence, the philosophy of traffic regulation shifted from anti-car to anti-accident. On October 13, 1913, The National Council for Industrial Safety opened a modest three-room headquarters in Chicago. The original emphasis was on the "industrial"—but in that same year, the Public Safety Commission of Chicago and Cook County reported that in July, 20 people had been killed by automobiles in the Windy City, 18 of them children. The commission launched an education program—with leaflets and stereopticon slides— in the schools and parks, and the new N.C.I.S. realized in its very first year that the motor car would have to be the subject of its most intense activity. In 1914 the organization's name was changed to the National Safety Council to permit a broadening of its scope.

The Council began to compile accident statistics from its first year; and the cold facts in black-on-white showed an unabating increase in motor vehicle deaths, both in numbers and in rate.

	Deaths	Rate Per 100,000 Pop.		Deaths	Rate Per 100,000 Pop.
1913	4,200	4.4	1922	15,300	13.9
1914	4,700	4.8	1923	18,400	16.5
1915	6,600	6.6	1924	19,400	17.1
1916	8,200	8.1	1925	21,900	19.1
1917	10,200	10.0	1926	23,400	20.1
1918	10,700	10.3	1927	25,800	21.8
1919	11,200	10.7	1928	28,000	23.4
1920	12,500	11.7	1929	31,200	25.7
1921	13,900	12.9	1930	32,900	26.7

The desire "to do something about it" was growing evident among Americans everywhere; but the equally strong urge to find unfettered freedom in an automobile seemed to negate the good being accomplished by education, driving regulations and new control techniques. In 1914 Detroit installed a manually-operated stop-and-go sign. In August that year an electrical traffic signal was put in operation at 105th and Euclid Avenue in Cleveland, Ohio. It was eight years later before Houston, Texas, had the first electrically inter-connected signals at 12 intersections. Schoolboy patrols were originated. The Ford Motor Company gave each automobile purchaser a card reminding him to Stop, Look and Listen at railroad crossings. In Philadelphia, as early as 1914, a "Miss Safety First" talked to 100,000 school children about street hazards. Magazines and newspapers carried don't-drink-when-you-drive cartoons; when Prohibition became a national reality (in name if not in effect), this emphasis was lessened considerably because no one was **supposed** to be imbibing. But the bootleggers in their big touring cars and bathtub-gin guzzlers in sporty rumble seat models continued to add to the highway carnage.

In 1924 the National Conference on Street and Highway Safety, chairmanned by Secretary of Commerce Herbert Hoover, authorized a committee to draft a uniform motor vehicle code for all 48 states. Two years later the legal package was presented and adopted by a second conference. Unfortunately, the individual states didn't react as quickly, but even so, the standardized code was a major achievement in the pursuit of effective nation-wide traffic regulation.

Die-hard horse-lovers, meanwhile, viewed the entire development with an I-told-you-so attitude. Now the nation would have to suffer for its folly in permitting the roads to be over-run with destructive mechanical monsters. Theirs was a neighing in the wilderness, however. The automobile had a solid wheel-hold on the American scene. No amount of crepe-hanging and finger-pointing could dislodge it. As one wag suggested: The motor car was a little like marriage; it had its good points and its bad. You simply had to enjoy the former and learn to live with the latter!

Most family albums contain photos like one above. Running boards made good posing seats. (Mr. and Mrs. Loyal Gunderson Collection).

AUTOMOBILES WERE NOT DANGEROUS when there were only a few of them but as numbers increased regulation was mandatory. Exuberance of drivers often added to problems. (American Automobile Association.).

NICOLLET AVENUE in Minneapolis in early 1920s was typical of big city streets, cluttered with conglomerate mixture of motor cars and trucks. The traffic policeman with manually-operated stop-and-go sign (above) seemed hardly adequate. There were also just enough horse-drawn vehicles (right) to complicate matters. (Photos Minnesota Historical Society).

TO KEEP UP WITH POPULACE law enforcement officers had to mechanize too. Police Department in San Jose, Calif. (above) selected 1907 Rambler as official car. It was especially impressive in local parades. (American Motors Corp.).

AUTOISTS AND STREET CAR MOTORMEN took turns aggravating and occasionally colliding with one another (opposite). Tram tracks were hazards particularly affecting vehicles with smooth-faced, solid rubber tires with little "give" to them. (Chas. Lytle Collection).

AS AUTOMOBILES GOT SPEEDIER, police officers on foot, bike or horse were at serious disadvantage. On his motorcycle (top right) Patrolman George A. Hunt was able to overtake law-violators in Rochester, N.Y. (The Smithsonian Institution). Pre-1900 photo (right) is identified as staged publicity shot in Chicago to promote Haynes-Apperson autos. Elwood Haynes, driving 1894 car he designed, seems little disturbed by incident. (American Automobile Assn.).

FROM EARLIEST DAYS automobile accidents have always attracted crowds of the morbidly curious (above). When mortality rates rose year by year, public began to believe pleasure cars could bring sadness too. (Harrah's Automobile Collection).

BECAUSE SPEED was not an overriding factor, many of early day auto accidents were not the gory smash-ups of a later generation and shoulderless roads accounted for numerous tip-overs. (Photos left, top to bottom—Denver Public Library Western Collection, 3; Harrah's Automobile Collection).

AUTOMOBILE was still in infancy when Life, magazine of that era (above), pointed out disastrous effects of mixing alcohol and gasoline. (Right) Williams Phelps Eno was pioneer in field of traffic regulations. As early as 1900 he submitted a traffic code for City of New York. (National Safety Council).

STREET TRAFFIC REGULATION

General Street Traffic Regulations — Special Street Traffic Regulations —Changes in Car Tracks and Curb Lines — City Planning —Road Signs — Articles and Addresses on Street Traffic —Federal License and Registration for Motor Cars —Civic Transportation — Police Administration —Police Horses — Equipment — Uniforms —How to Improve City Car Service

DEDICATED TO THE TRAFFIC SQUAD
OF THE
BUREAU OF STREET TRAFFIC
OF THE
POLICE DEPARTMENT
OF THE
CITY OF NEW YORK

BY WILLIAM PHELPS ENO

Author of Articles, Pamphlets and Addresses on Street Traffic Regulation and Civic Transportation—Folder of Rules for Driving furnished to and issued by the Police Department, Oct. 30, 1903—Articles and Sections of the Road Ordinance passed Dec. 14, 1903—Revised Folder and Poster of Rules for Driving and the Regulation of Street Traffic furnished to and issued by the Police Department, Feb. 22, 1908, and embodied in the Handbook of Police Regulations, Sept. 8, 1908—Revised Folder and Poster of Rules for Driving and the Regulation of Street Traffic issued by the Police Department, Feb. 8, 1909—Blue and White Traffic Signs in use and planned for, etc.

JULY, 1909

Published by THE RIDER AND DRIVER PUBLISHING CO.
1123 BROADWAY, NEW YORK

OLD-FASHIONED TOURING CARS like this right-hand drive Packard were roomy enough for a neighborhood party. (Pennsylvania Historical and Museum Collection).

WANDERLUST
... and Whoop-de-do!

Long before he became President, Woodrow Wilson (in 1906) unpolitically remarked that "nothing has spread socialistic feeling more than the use of the automobile . . . a picture of the arrogance of wealth."

He may have had a point at the time. Henry Ford had not yet conceived his "auto for the masses," so the motor car—unless it was home-made—was an expensive luxury which few could afford. But that situation was due to change rapidly. Installment buying entered the picture as early as 1905. Terms were tough in the beginning—at least 50 percent down and the rest "as soon as possible." The used car or trade-in concepts had not been established, so dealers —many of them totally new to the business—weren't much interested in long-term credit, especially when there was a chance that a nervous beginning driver might smash into a horse trough or hitching post before he'd gone a mile up the road.

Auto insurance was made available in Great Britain before the turn of the century, and the idea soon came to America. Insurance companies had a lot to learn, though, because—like so many other facets of the automotive development—there were no precedents to follow. Cars were often covered for their purchase price; and it wasn't until the deflationary period after World War I that insurers began to realize that some opportuniststic motorists were deliberately destroying their depreciated autos and collecting what they paid for them in the first place. Policies were forthwith revised to cover "actual value."

Gradually automobile ownership spread to the butcher, the baker, the lantern wick-maker. Car registrations spiraled upward, from a round figure of 8,000 in 1900, to 77,000 five years later. By 1910, 458,-000 passenger autos were legally recorded; there were 2,332,000 in 1915 and 8,132,000 in 1920. Americans at all socio-economic levels turned to the motor car for work and for whoop-de-do. Wanderlust became a national contagion and allied industries began to develop to accommodate this nomadic urge. Before 1907 there were no gas stations; by 1920 there were 15,000 of them. Less than ten years later, the total reached 121,500.

Most towns of any size had a hotel to put up the drummers and others who traveled mostly by rail. There was little thought about a tourist court for motorists. Way back in 1899, though, **McClure's Magazine** proposed asphalt streets and graveled country roads "with electric charging stations placed 20 miles apart with beer gardens and coffee houses where the chauffeurs and their guests could relax while their motor vehicles were being recharged."

As inter-city and cross-country travel began to attract the more venturesome, farmers found themselves with occasional unexpected over-night guests. A car would break down, a bridge would wash out, a wrong turn would be made—and the driver was stranded. A few dollar-conscious rural folks fixed up a cabin or two for such drop-in visitors. The idea developed slowly until there were tourist courts built especially as commercial ventures. In 1917 Samuel Conner Pandolfo—imaginative promoter, and con-artist extraordinary—built a "motor hotel" in St. Cloud, Minnesota, to accommodate visitors to his company. The American Automobile Association estimated that there were some 600 such enterprises in the U.S. by 1922. Standards were generally poor. Wise travelers turned the mattresses and looked in the crevasses for bedbugs. A few cabins had stoves; water usually had to be hauled in; and toilet facilities consisted of a communal two-, three- or four-holer.

As for charging off into the countryside, the pioneer motorists weren't much better off than Columbus when it came to maps and charts. They were almost non-existent. In the horse-dominated days, it was a general practice to establish tiny towns from seven to ten miles apart to serve farm-to-market needs. In familiar areas, the autoist could stumble from one community to another without getting lost—but when he ventured out on a cross-country trek through new territory, he had troubles galore. Road-markers were rare, and the advice of natives was questionable, since many of them hadn't traveled enough to know what roads existed outside their own townships.

In 1913 the Gulf Oil Company was the first U.S. petroleum firm to distribute free road maps. Meanwhile, the motorist who wanted to wander afar, became familiar with the Automobile Blue Book, an unusual publication officially sanctioned by the A.A.A. and devoted to the simple mission of instructing car operators how to get from-here-to-there. Since road signs were few and far between, the Blue Book contained highly detailed information on how to negotiate various routes from one town to the next.

For instance, if an automobilist wanted to travel from Sioux City, Iowa, to Omaha, Nebraska, in 1916, he went to Pierce and Fourth Streets in the former city where the Blue Book (Volume 5, Mississippi River to the Pacific Coast) indicated his speedometer mileage should be calculated at 0.0. From there the instructions were most explicit:

AFTER WORLD WAR I more and more motorists took to road, like this Texas couple who toured in do-it-themselves camper on Model T chassis. Curtain over windshield guaranteed privacy in over-night camp grounds. (Ford Archives, Henry Ford Museum).

Go south with trolley 1 block on Pierce, at Third Street, turn right. Cross railroad 0.4, curving left across long iron bridge over Missouri River 0.5 (toll 25 cents, a passenger car; 35 cents, 4 passenger car, and 5 cents additional for each passenger.) Jog right and immediately left, following trolley through South Sioux City 2.0; cross railroad 2.4; right hand road, turn right and immediately left around cemetery, still with trolley.

At 5.8 miles, four-corners, turn right with trolley through Dakota City. Cross railroad at station 6.3; four-corners with two churches at left, turn left at 9.1 miles. At end of road, turn right, turning left along bluffs farther on. Then turn left at church 15.8.

By then, the traveler was in Hosmer, Nebraska, and the instructions continued thusly all the way to Omaha. If he journeyed along by Blue Book, a driver was continually stopping to check the mileage to his next landmark. A road navigator with sharp eyes was a welcome companion.

The Blue Book plotted the entire nation from church steeple to water tower to the lone pine tree on the hill. The men who charted the trails for this vital traveler's guide knew the country intimately in tenth-of-a-mile segments. They were the nameless heroes of countless successful auto journeys in a period when there was little else to depend upon.

More and more the idea of providing various ser-

vices for motorists began to grow. The B. F. Goodrich Company, for instance, started a touring bureau in 1910 which became a major benefactor to pioneer travelers. It offered a guide publication similar to the Blue Book and gave away tour cards for inter-city trips (e.g., No. 718 described how to get from Indianapolis to Louisville, Kentucky). Cleveland was the starting point for the first tour mapped by Goodrich —to Buffalo, New York. Later, others were plotted until the firm had charted routes which crisscrossed the nation.

The biggest contribution made by B. F. Goodrich, though, was the company's erection of guide posts— round metal signs on 12-foot poles, each of which gave the name of the nearest town, the next large city and the ultimate destination of the particular route in the Goodrich guide book. Between 1910 and 1917, company crews erected thousands of signs on some 110,000 miles of U.S. roads. Counties and states began to assume a greater share of the road-marking responsibilities after World War I; till then, though, it was a haphazard proposition in which the driving public had to depend largely upon private promotions, like the Goodrich program, to keep tourists on the right road.

Automobile clubs, of course, played an important role in this regard. Members of the California State Automobile Association physically helped on road-building projects, manning shovels and operating split-log drags. In 1908 the organization started erecting directional and warning signs in and around the Bay Area. A San Francisco newspaper indicated how well the effort was received:

> Yesterday's pleasant weather brought out many automobile owners who took a spin through the park, over Parkside Boulevard into San Mateo County. To learn how much the automobilists appreciated the work of the Club, one had but to station himself near the signposts. As each car came along, the motorists would slow down, take a good look at the posts and then go on with a smile of satisfaction.

It didn't take much to improve the lot of the pioneer driver. He had started from scratch, so any little improvement seemed like a major accomplishment. Nothing was taken for granted—unless it was an autoist's assumption that he was going to suffer a few hardships each time he hit the open road.

But hit the road, he did! Picnics and scenic tours and fishing trips and visits to Aunt Jenny's lured an ever-increasing number of cars onto the nation's generally primitive highways. The auto activity gave impetus to the creation of new parks—local, regional and national—and spurred the development of those already in existence. The California State Automobile Association, for instance, fought for and won the right to operate motor vehicles in Yosemite National Park.

The touring obsession became so great that by 1917 sociologists began to worry about sexual and other such implications. One suggested that the reduced birth-rate in Kansas was attributable to the inability of young men to support both a wife and an automobile—and the misguided males were too frequently settling for the latter. Another advocated that the continual jostling and bumping of motor cars over rough, rutted roads was causing an alarming increase in mis-carriages—and thus affecting population. It was even seriously propounded that the automobile was upgrading the quality of U.S. babies. By expanding the radius of courtship, the researcher said, the horseless carriage had a beneficial effect on the problems of in-breeding and inter-marriage, especially in the southeastern states.

Be that as it may, the automobile certainly did bring Americans closer together. Because of it, the whole pattern of leisure and recreation changed. People wanted "to go somewhere"—and they did, laughing and singing and thoroughly perplexing the social theorists!

GIRL TOURIST finds new hero in Minnesota as Minnehaha Park guide changes her tire in 1925. (Minnesota Historical Society).

AS EARLY AS 1902 urge to See America was beginning to infect adventuresome motorists. Roads or no roads, most daring travelers sallied forth to enjoy nation's scenic beauties. Few, if any, motor cars preceded this Toledo (above) to rim of Grand Canyon. (Library of Congress).

THE NOMADIC URGE also spurred creation of some unusual mobile homes. All three of these homemade auto-houses (left) appeared at Denver's Overland Park in 1921. (Denver Public Library Western Collection).

FIRST DRIVER'S LICENSE in Denver, Colo., cost $1 and was issued in 1906 to William A. Hover (right). Other cities required engineers' permits to operate steamers which were classed as mobile boilers. (Denver Public Library Western Collection).

$1.00   No. 1

STATE OF COLORADO
BY AUTHORITY OF THE CITY AND COUNTY OF DENVER.

AUTOMOBILE PERMIT.

The Fire and Police Board of the City and County of Denver, to all who shall see these presents, Greeting:

KNOW YE, That Whereas, *Wm. A. Hover*
of *1507 La Fayette* Street, has made application for a permit to operate propel and drive an automobile, motor cycle or other similar vehicle within the City and County of Denver, and has otherwise complied with the ordinances of the City and County in this behalf,

THEREFORE, This is to certify that *Wm. A. Hover*
is permitted to operate, propel and drive an automobile, motor cycle or other similar vehicle within the City and County of Denver, subject to all the ordinances of the City and County now in force or which may hereafter be passed.

IN TESTIMONY WHEREOF, the Fire and Police Board, by its President, has hereunto set its hand this *Eleventh* day of *July* 190*6*

FIRE AND POLICE BOARD,

By _____
President.

THE HORSELESS CARRIAGE made picnics in country (above left) regular occurrences. And instead of staying in town for 4th of July parade, patriotic speeches and band concerts, people motored away and another old American tradition began to crumble. (American Automobile Assn.).

SMALL TOWN BOOSTER GROUPS formed auto cavalcades to visit neighbor towns, urge to parade incessant. Caravan above was organized in Volin, S.D. (Jorgen Bruget Collection) . . . Below, Mr. and Mrs. Paul Kasdorf (center seat) enjoy spin in Papa Kasdorf's new 1909 Rambler on their wedding day in Blue Island, Ill. Auto charivari, with tin cans and old shoes tied behind, became social custom. (American Motors Corporation).

HISTORICAL SITES received new emphasis with advent of auto. People went places they read about, such as Old Round Tower (above left) at Fort Snelling, Minn. (Minnesota Historical Society). And (above right) an inventive Georgia camper devised this unique trailer house. When traveling roof could be lowered to level of 1921 Essex. (American Motors Corp.).

IN SALT LAKE CITY (right) rooters for University of Utah football team whooped it up on pioneer hard-tired tour bus. It was an era of motorized monkeyshines. (Denver Public Library Western Collection).

AUTO WAS BOON TO WOOING (below). One sociologist even said it improved American blood lines (see text). (Library of Congress).

AUTO PARADE (above) was feature event of 1909 Pratt, Kansas, County Fair— an exciting harbinger of things to come. (Library of Congress) . . . Minneapolis Elks decorated auto for little parade whoop - de - do. (Minnesota Historical Society).

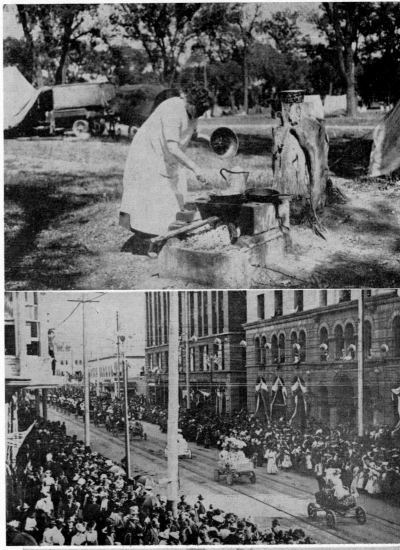

MOTOR CAR OWNERS JUMPED at chance to join parades. Floral designed autos were featured in 1901 Festival of Mountain and Plain (right top) and Overland Park (right center)—both views in Denver. (Denver Public Library Western Collection).

1904 AAA-SPONSORED CARAVAN from New York City (right) to Louisiana Purchase Exposition in St. Louis was one of most ambitious junkets up to that time. It led Charles J. Glidden to propose tours bearing his name. (Library of Congress).

ROAD MARKERS were few and far between when 1905 Rambler was new. This unusual picture (top left) was taken by L. L. Peddinghaus, Marietta, Ohio, jeweler and photography enthusiast. He rigged up automatic shutter on camera, jumped in behind steering wheel before exposure was made. (American Motors Corp.). In center photo left, tourists are shown in Washington's Mt. Rainier National Park. (Chester Gibbon Collection).

BEFORE DAYS OF FREE MAPS and government-marked roads, B. F. Goodrich Company Tourist Bureau was motorist's best friend. Firm's guide post trucks (below) roamed nation, erecting directional signs, keeping route books and tour cards current. (The B. F. Goodrich Company).

TWO RAMBLERS—1908 Model 34A (above center) and 1904 Model J (above right)—offered transportation for motor-minded nimrod. Automobiles took sportsmen farther from city to better hunting and fishing locations far from business cares. (Photos American Motors Corp.).

LURE OF OPEN ROAD (right and below) came with the automobile. Normally stay-put Americans began to explore country from one end to the other, including tiny tots and family pets. (Photos W. S. Campbell Collection, Div. of Manuscripts, U. of Oklahoma Library).

DRIVER of this electric hansom cab had bird's-eye view of traffic. (The Smithsonian Institution).

AT WORK
... and At War

Even before it had shed its bicycle wheels and whip socket, the horseless carriage was put to work. The idea that it would be merely a rich man's toy or a pleasure-seeker's folly was advanced by its detractors—but the men involved in its creation visualized for it an endless variety of productive uses.

While the Duryeas, Ford, Alexander Winton and other American pioneers were still working on their original models, motorized taxicabs, omnibuses, freight lorries and delivery vans were already proving their worth in Europe. A similar pattern soon established itself in the United States, with electric and steam models getting a slight jump on gas-powered vehicles.

Before Henry Ford had pried enough bricks loose to get his Quadricycle out of the Bagley Avenue fuel shed, the Charles E. Woods firm in Chicago was manufacturing light electric delivery wagons. In Providence, Rhode Island, a department store had a horse van converted into a steam-propelled vehicle. From one end of the country to the other, there was a curious interest in the development of motorized commercial transport. By 1900 at least three sets of brothers—who were to become leaders in the industry —were producing their first work vehicles: the Stanleys and Whites with small steam delivery trucks and the Macks, a gas-operated sightseeing bus.

The development of the motor truck is another

AUTOMOBILES WERE BOON TO SALESMEN, making it possible for them to make more calls and expand territories. Here a squad of "Texas Hustlers" were poised for assault on far-flung customers. (Div. of Manuscripts, University of Oklahoma Library).

story (see **This Was Trucking,** Bibliography); but the so-called passenger or pleasure cars were also put to work. Quick to recognize the value of the automobile were the medical doctors in an era when the physician went to his patients and not the other way around. Saddlebag surgeons were generally overjoyed to trade their steeds for Franklins, Ramblers, Molines or Locomobiles. The auto permitted doctors to make their rounds quicker, to treat more people and to have a little time left over for study. With horse-and-buggy, they were often on the road more than at the bedside, which was an obvious waste of training and talent.

For people who lived in the hinterlands, the motor car provided a major change in communications. Rural Free Delivery was inaugurated on five routes in West Virginia on October 1, 1896, just a few days after Alexander Winton introduced his first experimental two-seater in Cleveland, and not quite four months after Henry Ford unveiled his Quadricycle. The Duryea Motor Wagon Company built 13 cars that year, the first quantity production of gas-mobiles in the U.S. The net effect was that R.F.D. and automobiles grew up together.

Of necessity, horse-drawn vehicles were first used on the mail routes because of cost, availability and condition of the roads. By 1899, though, the U.S. Post Office Department began experimenting with motor cars for mail collection in Buffalo, New York; Cleveland, Ohio, and Washington, D.C. The success of these and subsequent tests spurred interest in the automobile for delivery service, and soon after the turn of the century, a limited number of rural mail carriers switched to motorized equipment. There were objections, of course, and general acceptance didn't come overnight—but by 1906 the **Scientific American** reported:

> . . . Postmaster-General Cortelyou has issued an order sanctioning the use of automobiles and motor cycles where the roads are maintained in good condition and the physical aspects of the country are favorable to the use of such cars. As a precautionary measure the Department reserves the right to require rural carriers to discontinue the use of horseless vehicles, and resume the service of their routes in ordinary vehicles, if complaint is made of unsatisfactory service arising from the use of autos.

Politically the Postmaster General left himself an "out" if the route patrons were not happy, or if too many horses were disturbed by the new arrangement. But the economic factors so greatly favored automobile delivery that it was almost indefensible not to use it. Also, it was in 1906 that the Waltham Manufacturing Company of Waltham, Massachusetts, designed the 1-cylinder friction-drive Orient buckboard specifically for postal work. It was fitted with a mackintosh buggy top, and mounted in front of the driver was a mail case divided into pigeon-hole compartments. This imaginative approach by a manufacturer focused additional attention on the automobile as a medium to improve and expand Rural Free Delivery. By 1913, when parcel post service was begun, the auto was well established.

Imagination was a major factor in the adaptation of the motor car to other commercial assignments.

Salesmen, for instance, saw in the auto a way to increase their daily calls and to add to their territories. In the cities they had been limited by foot, streetcar, bicycles or horse travel. The drummers who wandered afar had to use the railroads—and then hire a horse-and-buggy at a livery stable if they wanted to cover any ground at each location. In the early days the automobile was also an attraction which helped the salesman draw a crowd and call attention to the fact that he had arrived to do business. The more ingenious peddlers began immediately to advertise their wares with signs on the car doors or specially built promotion gimmicks mounted somewhere or other on the vehicle. In 1914 the **Ford Times** published what it called the salesman's lament: "If I had a Ford car, I could cover more territory, see my customers regularly and increase my orders."

Other manufacturers began to promote their products creatively. The Brush Runabout Company advertised directly to the businessman: "You can get to your office quicker than by street car, cheaper than by train, and the fresh morning air will fit you for the day's work." In 1908 Sears, Roebuck and Company used a similar approach:

> The Sears is the car for the business man who has not yet "made his pile" and cannot afford to be charged with extravagance by his business associates . . . whose business would grow faster if he could get through with more work in the same number of hours.

So it went, a continuing quest for new customers and new uses for the motor vehicle. Policemen and firefighters switched to automobiles and trucks designed for their specific needs; traffic officers especially required speedy cars and motorcycles to be effective against the reckless drivers they could never catch afoot or on bikes. Telephone and telegraph companies figured out how to use the Model T magneto for field testing their lines. The Day Automobile Company came up with a unique idea, the Day Utility Car which in less than a minute could be converted from a touring car into a delivery wagon be detaching the rear seat. "Farmers, gardeners and tradesmen have demanded such a car for years," the firm's advertising said.

Farmers, of course, were particularly wooed by the auto manfacturers. If they could be sold on the motor car, they constituted a huge market; they would be a strong political force in the development of non-urban roads; and, once convinced, they might drop their anti-auto attitude which reflected itself in legal restrictions and other activities detrimental to motoring.

There was an era—generally from 1907 through 1911—when a distinct style of automobile was in its hey-day. The so-called "highwheelers" were, in effect, mechanized buggies; they marked a last-gasp stand of carriage makers who found themselves caught between two modes of transportation. The highwheelers, however, proved to be effective transitional vehicles in the pre-Model T period. They were inexpensive to buy and operate; they were relatively uncomplicated; and their narrow, hard-tired wheels were adapted to the deep-rutted rural roads of the day.

Many farmers became rabid auto enthusiasts

through ownership of these short-lived vehicles. There were 15 makes of highwheelers in 1907, a peak of 41 in 1909 and only 9 two years later. Still, the Schacts, Kiblingers, Holsmans, IHC Auto Buggies, Blacks, Duers, Reliable Daytons, McIntyres, Jewels and three score others played an important interim role in the development of the modern automobile. They made it possible for farmers to bring fresh cream, milk, butter, eggs, produce and other perishables into town profitably—to their advantage and that of the city dweller whose dinner table was thus favorably enhanced.

In the meantime, another important use for motorized vehicles was being developed: military transport. The U.S. Army bought three electric units as early as 1899, but the philosophy of mechanization was slow in coming. At that time the military was dominated by elderly horse-soldiers whose active careers dated back to the Civil War. They were, with few exceptions, romanticists and non-progressives who saw little need to disturb the comfortable status quo. Their laggardly acceptance of the automobile and motor truck was almost a disastrous misjudgment when related to the U.S. effort in World War I.

The persistency of a young officer—Capt. Alexander A. Williams—who finally convinced his superiors to give motor vehicles a chance to prove themselves in military logistics, and the escapades of a Mexican bandit named Pancho Villa helped avert a potentially tragic lack of preparation. Captain Williams showed the worth of trucks in a gruelling 1,509-mile-test from Washington, D.C., to Fort Benjamin Harrison, Indiana, via Atlanta, Georgia, in 1912—but still the brass was slow to act. Finally, in 1916, when Villa made his historic raid on Columbus, New Mexico,

and the Punitive Expedition under General John J. Pershing was mobilized, the military hierarchy was dragged into the twentieth century in spite of itself.

Before the 11-month campaign was over, Pershing had requested and received hundreds of motor cars and trucks—of more than 120 different makes with the resultant melange of spare parts and dissimilar operating procedures. This was particularly chaotic since the army had virtually no trained drivers or mechanics when the first vehicle arrived on the Mexican border.

The fantastic mess accomplished a positive result, however. The value of mechanization was proved, and the importance of standardization was obvious. Even though the American Expeditionary Force was woefully lacking in motor vehicles when its first units departed for France in 1918, still the situation would have been much, much worse without the experience of the pursuit of the irrepressible Villa.

Trucks, command cars, ambulances and other specialty vehicles demonstrated their worth in war-time, in spite of the difficulties of supply, maintenance and road conditions. Military needs spurred production at home; literally thousands of mechanics and drivers were trained; and when the Armistice was declared, long queues of vehicles went on the surplus list, with the trucks especially being utilized by state highway departments in the building of more and better roads for an auto-conscious nation.

At work and at war, the motor car had proved itself valiantly. As a matter of fact, the gasless Sundays and other restrictions of a war-time economy had brought an end to the expression "pleasure car." From that period on, the auto and truck became recognized as necessities of a new society.

HEAVY HAULING on solid tires in Denver. (Denver Public Library Western Collection).

U.S. POST OFFICE DEPARTMENT bought its first motor vehicle in 1899 on experimental b a s i s. Trucks proved particularly efficient for mail collection and transport between railroad stations and post offices. In Milwaukee (above) Johnson Service Company built 8 custom steamers to fulfill postal contract there. (Johnson Service Company).

IN 1906 WALTHAM (MASS.) MANUFACTURING COMPANY i n t r o-duced Orient buckboard for postal delivery. It had mail case with pigeon-hole compartments directly in front of driver. That same year Postmaster General approved auto delivery "if too many patrons do not object." (Library of Congress).

MODEL T FORD was undoubtedly most versatile auto ever created. It was adapted, rebuilt, remodeled, cut down and souped up to fit every imaginable kind of assignment. This special winter gear (right top) was marketed by accessory manufacturer. (Ford Motor Company Archives).

CUSTOM-BUILT AMBULANCES (right center and bottom) made appearance in first decade of 1900 and played major role in World War I. (Photos Johnson Service Company).

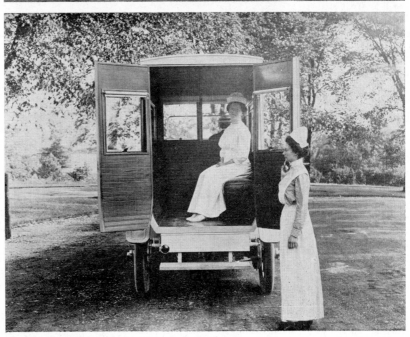

BRIG. GEN. PERSHING (left) led Punitive Expedition against Pancho Villa in 1916-17, his experience with motor vehicles there helping avoid transportation debacle in World War I. Jeffery Quad truck was one of many makes which saw service on Mexican border. (Below) Eddie Rickenbacker, America's leading ace of World War I, drove this 1917 Hudson in France. The AEF used almost 300 different makes and models of motor vehicles before Armistice. (Photos American Motors Corp.).

AS MOTOR CARS, TRUCKS AND BUSES evolved, some unusual work vehicles were included in family tree. An International Harvester truck (top left) was adapted to railroad service, complete with cow-catcher, while Allis-Chalmers made giant tractor-truck for short time (top center). . . . In 1915 at San Francisco Pan-Pacific Exposition Wells Fargo Company was feted with special day. Historic freighting firm had switched to motor vehicles, like this Federal truck (top right) to compete in new age of transport. (Photos left to right, International Harvester Company, Allis-Chalmbers, Wells Fargo Bank History Room).

DELIVERY TRUCKS of all shapes and sizes were built as motor cars proved practical. At first limited mostly to in-city runs, highway improvements allowed operation on longer routes. 1905 Rambler (below) showed considerable advancement over tiller-steered van (right) which first delivered goods in Denver in 1900. (Photo below, American Motors Corp.; right, Denver Public Library Western Collection).

BUSES WERE DEVELOPED concurrently with autos and trucks. At first used largely for sightseeing (top) they were adapted, about time of World War I, to hauling factory personnel. Later, in 20s, with improved highways and vehicles, inter-city passenger service (above) became common practice, particularly where railroads did not operate. Both Delco, above, and Goodyear buses, below, were built on White chassis. (Top, Denver Public Library Western Collection; center, Delco Products Div. General Motors; bottom, The Goodyear Tire and Rubber Company).

PHYSICIAN'S NUMBER

JOHNSON HIGH-RIGGER (above left) was specifically designed to service streetcar lines. Johnson Service Company, Milwaukee, Wisc., built both steam and gas trucks and autos from 1901 to 1912. (Johnson Service Company) . . . Medical doctors (above right) were often first in communities to have automobiles and able to travel farther, faster and see more patients than by horse and buggy. (Harrah's Automobile Collection) . . . Short-lived high wheelers (below) were built to give farmers vehicles for deep-rutted rural roads and make continuing market for carriage makers. (Left below, John A. Conde Collection; right, South Dakota Historical Society).

CARS AND TRUCKS WENT TO WAR in 1917-18—and helped celebrate end of it. Armistice Day parade in Denver, Colo. (left column) featured giant portrait of Gen. Pershing, hundreds of American flags and expressive sign: "To hell with the Kaiser!" (Photos Denver Public Library Western Collection).

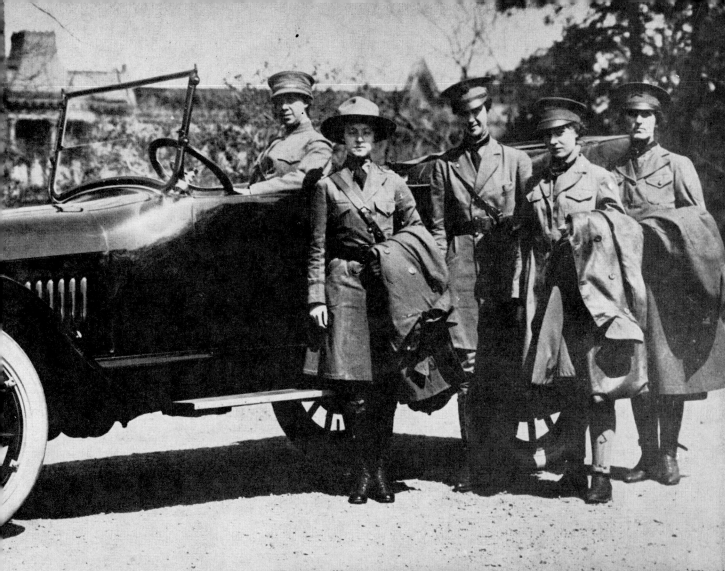

STAFF CARS like 1917 Chandler (above) were vital part of World War I fleet. Conflict forced technological development and automotive age moved ahead faster. (John A. Conde Collection).

TRUCKS OF ALL SIZES (right) and design became symbols of new motor-mode of transportation follolling World War I. Universal availability of vehicles, trained personnel, improved roads, automotive parts and fuel spurred rapid development of vast industry. (Denver Public Library Western Collection).

IN 1899 THE SIGNAL CORPS ordered 3 electric vehicles from Woods Motor Vehicle Company of Chicago. It marked beginning of military experimentation by U.S. Army. Progress was slow but by WWI Signal Corps could boast of such specialty units as Nash Quad radio tractor (above)—(American Motors Corp.) . . . Winton wagonette (below) was one of earliest service motor vehicles. (The Smithsonian Institution).

MOTOR CAR GOT INTO POLITICS (above) even before it switched from tiller to steering wheel. This one was used to campaign for Denver Mayor Robert W. Speer in 1904. (Denver Public Library Western Collection) . . . Success of Chevrolet and other cars in low-price field caused Henry Ford, in 1927, to sack his Tin Lizzie and create Model A. In Stratford, N.J. this super-long carrier (below) was loaded down with new Chevvies. (General Motors Truck and Coach Division).

HAND THAT ROCKED CRADLE occasionally turned to adjusting carburetor in embryonic days of motoring. (The Smithsonian Institution).

The Smell of
PERFUME and PETROL

It was inevitable that when the first automobile sputtered forth, it wouldn't be long before the ladies would be clamoring to get behind the steering tiller.

For them it was a transitional period, too. The mores of the Victorian period were very much in evidence, but militant suffragettes were preaching female emancipation. In the 1890s it was still most unladylike for a woman to be a doctor, to show her ankles or to tinker with things mechanical.

Still, there were the front-runners—the customs-be-damned gals—who jumped the traces into areas where the majority of their gender feared to tread. The advent of the motor car provided just one more avenue to freedom, and the gutsier ladies took advantage of it.

Since the earliest cars were generally owned by the more affluent, the mesdames of high society took the lead in the effort to prove that the hand that rocked the cradle could also adjust a carburetor. **The Automobile Magazine** in the fall of 1899 announced that the horsey set of Newport, Rhode Island, had switched to automobiles and that the women had insisted upon driving their own rigs. The first **chauffeuse** (that's what the magazine called her) to appear in public was Miss Daisy Post, a niece of Mrs. Frederick Vanderbilt; she was joined shortly thereafter by Mrs. Herman Oelrichs and Mrs. William K. Vanderbilt.

Then the publication went on to describe the first driving experience of Mrs. Stuyvesant Fish that summer:

> Mrs. Fish, with Miss Greta Pomeroy by her side, started to take the machine around the grounds next day. It was their intention to stick closely to the drives and crosswalks, but the automobile saw a stone wall and made for it, head on. The automobile won, and a large section of the stone wall fell with a thud. The motor shook itself free from the debris, and all went well for a while; but soon the automobile proceeded to lay low a clump of choice shrubbery on the lawn. For the next half hour Mrs. Fish had a more or less exciting time, and then came the climax. The carriage finally dashed against the steps of the villa, whereupon there was an awful, sudden stop, a crash and a snap, and the side of the automobile gave way, and the day's lesson necessarily came to an end.

Without knowing it, Mrs. Fish may thus have been the indirect originator of the epithetic expression, "woman driver," which men have used derisively ever since. In the pioneering period there were plenty of male motorists who were no better than Mrs. Fish on their first try—and some who were worse. History records numerous instances when panic-stricken he-men lost control of their automobiles and frantically shouted "Whoa! whoa!"—a plea which their horseless carriages were unable to heed.

Among the first women autoists was Anne Rainsford French of Washington, D.C. Her father—William Bates French, one of the capital city's most noted physicians—was a horse-hater from the word "giddap," and when he had the chance to buy a steam Locomobile for $600 in 1899, he could hardly wait to get his wallet out. Since his wife was somewhat fearful of the new contraption, Doctor French agreed to include his daughter as a motoring companion—but not as a driver.

At first Anne merely accompanied her father on his rounds, holding an umbrella over his head if it happened to be raining or sitting pert and feminine beside him when the weather was nice. Finally, however, she developed the courage to ask permission to operate the car herself. At first the doctor's reaction was entirely negative, but when she argued that the value of an assistant chauffeur—one who could keep the steam up while the physician was busy on a house call, for instance—the father relented and agreed to give her lessons.

First, though, she had to get her hands dirty. The doctor required that she be able to disassemble, clean and restore the engine, and for her final test, he shook up all the parts in a blanket and told her to put them back together. She passed admirably, and only then did her father begin to teach her to drive. At that time, an operator's license was unknown in the District of Columbia, but with the increasing number of motor vehicles—especially steamers—the commissioners decided to do something about it. They decided that the French's Locomobile was, in effect, a portable boiler and, therefore, those who operated it must have a steam engineer's license. Needless to say, they were somewhat taken aback when a pretty girl appeared before them to request examination for the $3 permit. Again her persistence was effective, and on March 22, 1900, she was awarded her Steam Engineer's License, Locomobile Class, which made her one of the earliest licensed woman drivers in the United States.

Just what young lady first operated a motor car is still a matter of historic conjecture. Mrs. John Howell Phillips of Chicago was said to have been licensed two months earlier than Miss French. That same

DOZEN BONNETED BEAUTIES posed for posterity in this vintage touring car in Denver. Only most daring ladies tinkered with engines, majority preferring passenger role—in fashionable dusters and motor chapeaux. (Denver Public Library Western Collection).

year in the Windy City 13-year-old Jeannette Lindstrom received License No. 322, and it was claimed that she had already been driving for two years. In 1899 Mrs. Mary Landon, the entire office force of the Haynes-Apperson Automobile Company, apparently piloted one of the firm's vehicles across town after first reading the instruction sheet which went with each auto. Upon her successful arrival at the factory, Elmer Apperson crowned her achievement with a simple, "Well, I'll be damned!"

During the next decade the ladies showed considerable interest in automobiles, not only as passengers, but as operators, too. The greatest preference of female drivers, though, was for the uncomplicated, odorless and less messy electrics. Restricted as they were by multiple petticoats and floor-sweeping dresses, they were unable to react rapidly without tangling their legs in a dozen ells of underclothing. Possibly that's what happened to Mrs. Newton J. Cuneo of New York, the only woman driver in the first Glidden Tour of 1905. She was sailing along smoothly when another auto stalled ahead of her on a narrow bridge. She was slow to apply the brakes, rear-ended the other car and tipped her own into the creek.

In 1909 Mrs. John R. (Alice) Ramsey and three women companions (her two sisters-in-law, Nettie Powell and Margaret Atwood, and Miss Hermine Johns) piloted a Maxwell touring car from New York City to San Francisco in 53 days. That was a test of courage and stamina of which any man could have been proud. In the process they proved themselves capable of keeping their car in operation, changing tires and finding their way on unmarked roads. They traveled by Blue Book as far as they could; the Far West editions hadn't been printed yet. Probably their greatest hardship was living out of a suitcase—one per gal—for the entire journey. Fortunately, the Maxwell company hired an advance man— John D. Murphy, automobile editor of the **Boston Herald**—to precede the women by train. He made the necessary hotel accommodations and checked on the gasoline supply for their extra-large 20-gallon fuel tank.

The emergence of the internal combustion engine as the most preferred mode of automotive power kept many women from the driver's seat in the earlier days, not because they couldn't handle the vehicles once they got moving but because they simply weren't strong enough to hand-crank the motors into action. The wrist-demolishing crank, of course, wasn't particularly popular, even with the most muscular; consequently, the quest to eliminate it was of major concern to manufacturers. Rope, gas and spring starters were introduced, but all proved ineffective. In 1911 the Amplex auto had a compressed air starter which was a little better than earlier air-type models. Finally a year later, Cadillac adopted an electric device developed by Charles F. Kettering of the Dayton Engineering Laboratories Company (Delco), and a new era of motoring dawned.

The self-starter did away with the ungodly physical effort required to begin a motor trip. No longer was it necessary for a man to be around when a lady wanted to take a spin in her Mercer, her Parry or her Abbott-Detroit. Cranking was dangerous, too, and a tragic experience in 1910 emphasized the point. Bryon T. Carter — after whom the Cartercar was named—had stopped to help a woman driver whose car had stalled. The crank kicked back as Carter was trying to start the auto, striking him in the jaw with such force that he ultimately died of the blow. No wonder the Kettering invention (which was based on a tiny electric motor made originally for cash registers) was so gratefully received by all motorists, men and women alike!

By this time it was no longer considered unfeminine for a woman to drive. Queen Victoria of England had died in 1901, and gradually the symbols of her moralistic influence began to fade. In 1914 the Saxon Motor Car Corporation took advertising advantage of the fact that two well known suffragettes—Mrs. Alice Snitzer Burke and Miss Nell Richardson—toured the United States in one of their autos. The promotion copy read:

> For five months they sped from city to city, from town to town, following a definite schedule, covered 10,000 miles and were never late once. Over both the Eastern and Western mountain ranges, across the arid deserts of Nevada and California as well as the great waste stretches of Utah, and through mud hub deep, went the Saxon Roadster surmounting every obstacle of road and weather . . . Throughout the entire journey Mrs. Burke and Miss Richardson handled the wheel, changing tires when necessary, and personally gave all the slight service that was needed to keep the car in perfect condition.

Two years later Miss Nell Leon was to begin a more ambitious project, and in the ensuing decade she drove the same Buick more than 400,000 miles, through all 48 states and 37 foreign countries. After that, the distaff side could hardly ask for concessions from their male counterparts on the road. The Four Wheel Drive Corporation, to prove how simple their product was to manipulate, hired Miss Luella Bates to drive a three-ton truck from Clintonville, Wisconsin, to the New York Auto Show of 1919. She then took the same vehicle on a transcontinental tour.

Needless to say, the ladies added a new dimension to motoring. Fashion became a factor right from the beginning. As early as 1899, the women of Newport went to Paris for gowns of silk jersey designed for freedom of action when a brake pedal had to be jammed on hurriedly. The dresses cost $500, a fact which no doubt helped Woodrow Wilson relate the earliest auto-ownership to "the arrogance of wealth." But even as the socio-economic level of autoists decreased, the ladies continued to insist upon proper motoring toggery. Fashionable dusters, scarves, veils, chapeaus and gauntlet-style gloves were a must. (Men wore special togs, too, and sported fancy automobile watch fobs.) Before windshields became standard equipment, goggles had to be part of the attire. Some ladies wore large face-covering bonnets—like beekeepers' hats—with a glass window to see through, or they carried "auto lorgnettes," tiny hand-windshields which they held in front of their faces to keep dust and bugs out of their eyes.

It was all part of an exciting era, when age-old customs, styles and personal restrictions began to crumble, and—for better or for worse—the automobile played an influencing role in the change. The status of the so-called weaker sex was considerably improved as the shackles born of Old Country thinking were loosed. On August 26, 1920, Tennessee became the 36th state to ratify the 19th Amendment, and the suffragettes' grand cause was achieved.

Equal rights became a reality, and a slogan of the Pullman auto—made in York, Pennsylvania—had a special, jubilant meaning: "Tailored for Her Majesty, the American Woman."

WHEN EXPOSURE TO ELEMENTS was overcome and self-starter eliminated rigors of cranking, the automobile had even greater appeal to women. Autos shown here are 1921 Skelton Seasonette (above) and 1920 Haynes (opposite). (John A. Conde Collection).

BIG BONNETS AND BIG SMILES characterized these Denver women (right column) in variety of early day autos. (Photos Denver Public Library Western Collection).

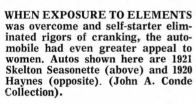

TEACHING MILADY TO DRIVE (above left), whether in Paige roadster or top-heavy electric, was another frustration of era. A doctor in Washington, D.C. even required his daughter to re-assemble torn-down engine before he would permit her to get behind wheel. . . . Ladies generally preferred electrics like 1908 Kimball (above center) because they were clean, odorless and simple to operate. As long as they got back to garage before batteries ran down there was little to worry about. (Photos left and right, The Smithsonian Institution; center, Pennsylvania Historical and Museum Commission).

PIONEER AUTO AND WOMAN'S SUFFRAGE movement were contemporaries—both symbols of freedom for distaff side. Ladies exhibited their self-sufficiency by operating motor cars of all types like 1905 Marvel (below left), massive Packard (below center) and washboard-nosed White Steamer (below right) —(Photos left to right, Pennsylvania Historical and Museum Commission, 2; John A. Conde Collection).

ONE INTREPID FEMALE TRAV-
ELER was Nell Leon (above) who
in 10 years drove same 1916 Buick
more than 400,000 miles through all
48 states and 37 foreign countries.
(Texaco Archives).

LADY MOTORISTS STUDY MAP
posted in Denver's Overland Park
(left). During period when travelers
toured by Blue Book, women often
functioned as navigators, checking
instructions and looking for appropriate landmarks. (Denver Public
Library Western Collection).

FOR LADIES who preferred to ride
and not drive, there were always
such socially proper automobiles as
this Welch Landau (above) manufactured by Welch Motor Car Company, Pontiac, Mich. (John A. Conde
Collection).

KANSAS LADIES drove local products like Brown Brothers creation
(right center) built in Manhattan
and Great Smith (bottom) made in
Topeka. (Photos The Kansas State
Historical Society).

PRESIDENT COOLIDGE motored down Nicollet Ave. in Minneapolis when he attended 1925 Norse-American Centennial celebration. (Minnesota Historical Society).

CHIEFS and INDIANS
on wheels

When Chief Geronimo and Buffalo Bill Cody got down off their horses and moved in behind a steering wheel, it was proof positive that the automobile had truly arrived. And starting with McKinley, the American Presidents adopted the motor car for parades, official trips and campaign tours; even Woodrow Wilson relented from his earlier anti-auto stand.

Celebrities, of course, helped the manufacturers sell their machines; testimonial advertising became as important as tour and race publicity. When the first White House fleet was assembled in a converted carriage house in 1908, three companies had scored a merchandising coup. A White Steamer, a Baker Electric and two Pierce-Arrows had been selected to serve President Taft and his staff, and, needless to say, the manufacturers took full advantage of this presidential recognition.

Thomas Edison, who insisted that the horse was the most inefficient motor ever conceived, made points for the automobile industry every time he appeared in a car—usually an electric one, of course. In the first ten years of the new century, the automobile developed from a hopeful concept to a practical, commercial reality, and its acceptance by people of consequence helped achieve this rapid, far-reaching success.

The automotive industry also created its own celebrities. Men like Barney Oldfield, Fred Marriott, E. G. "Cannonball" Baker, Louis Chevrolet and others were well known for their driving feats. Prize fighters, baseball players and stars of the silent screen were pictured with motor cars whenever possible. Even Sidney Smith, the creator of "Andy Gump," and his $16,000 custom-built Locomobile were well publicized.

PRESIDENT TAFT (second from right) was auto devotee, and during his administration 4-car White House fleet was purchased. It included massive White Steamer which was highly impressive in parade appearances. (Eaton, Yale and Towne, Inc.).

PRESIDENT WOODROW WILSON, who once condemned automobile as symbol of "the arrogance of wealth," came to accept it as necessary part of new age. (Chas. Lytle Collection).

During an era when hundreds of manufacturers were vying for the same potential customers, the importance of good promotion could not be overestimated. When the King of Siam bought a 1903 Baker Electric trimmed with white pigskin, ivory and gold, the company made the most of it. King Alfonso XIII of Spain drove a Duesenberg which added luster to the name of the two German brothers, Fred and August, whose first car—the Mason—was built in Iowa in 1906. Packard was proud of the fact that Czar Nicholas II of Russia fitted a Twin Six with skis and caterpillar tracks to operate over Siberian snows.

Louis Chevrolet was a recognized designer, but no doubt William C. Durant was also interested in his racing name as well as the auto he created. Likewise, Barney Everitt, who had made a sizeable fortune with the E.M.F. car (predecessor of the later-day Studebaker), attempted to capitalize on the fame of America's World War I flying ace, Captain Eddie Rickenbacker, by investing in an auto of the same name. After one successful year, the Rickenbacker plummeted from the industrial skies like a German

Fokker in the famous flyer's gunsights, while the Chevrolet succeeded so well that it forced Henry Ford to scrap his previously unchallenged Model T. It took more than a name on the radiator to insure a car's future. The Studebaker Corporation learned the same lesson when it introduced a low-priced model named for Knute Rockne, the highly acclaimed football coach of Notre Dame. It lasted about as long as the Geronimo, built by the Geronimo Motor Company, Enid, Oklahoma.

Chiefs of state, Indians, opera stars, comedians, cowboy heroes like Tom Mix, generals like "Black Jack" Pershing and many other noteworthy individuals helped sell automobiles simply by appearing in them.

It was an era of gullibility, of hero worship and of great competition. When it was over, only a handful of manufacturers remained—and against the backdrop of history, it is obvious now that success could never be assured, no matter how many U. S. Presidents rode in a particular automobile nor how famous the nameplate it bore.

PRESIDENT WILLIAM HOWARD TAFT believed in automobile enough for White House to own Baker Electric, White Steamer and 2 Pierce-Arrows. To protect him his regular chauffeur often carried pistol in gauntlet. This historical photo below was taken in 1910 when Taft visited home of Abraham Lincoln in Springfield, Ill. Auto was 1910 Springfield built in that city from 1907 to 1912. (Top, International Harvester; bottom, John A. Conde Collection).

CAPT. LOWELL SMITH (top left), famed round-the-world flyer of U.S. Army, posed in first Chrysler 6 Roadster in 1924. Note rumble seat. (Chrysler Corp.); Gary Cooper (top center) with 1929 Packard Eight. (Harrah's Automobile Collection); Tom Mix (top right) with 1921 Leach Roadster. (Stanley K. Yost Collection).

THOMAS A. EDISON had this electric phaeton custom-built by Studebaker, second of 1,841 electrics manufactured by company from 1902 to 1912. Edison was vocal exponent of such vehicles but was never able to develop battery capable of giving them range and speed necessary to compete with gasoline-operated models. (Studebaker Corp.)

BARNEY OLDFIELD (opposite center) was celebrity long after his racing days. For a time there was an Oldfield auto manufactured in Los Angeles, but like Rickenbacker, it lasted only about 5 years. (Harrah's Automobile Collection).

IN TRADITION OF HER ART, Madame Ernestine Schumann-Heink (opposite bottom), opera diva, rode in her 1930 Cadillac V-16. By this time, obviously, hardships of early day motoring were far behind. (John A. Conde Collection).

BUFFALO BILL CODY (above) momentarily deserted saddle for driver's seat of this National touring car—manufactured in Indianapolis, Ind. from 1900 to 1924. (Denver Public Library Western Collection) . . . William Jennings Bryan, (below) fiery free-silver orator, campaigned in 1907 Rambler. (The Kansas State Historical Society).

COMEDIANS HARRY LAUDER in 1913 Hudson (left) and Eddie Cantor in vintage truck (above), like other celebrities of their era, were indirect promoters of motor vehicles each time they appeared in them. (Photos, left—American Motors Corp., above—The Free Library of Philadelphia) . . . Theodore Roosevelt loved horses but accepted motor car. He was photographed (below) during parade in St. Paul, Minn. in 1912. (Minnesota Historical Society).

CHIEF GERONIMO, wearing top hat (above), posed in Locomobile in 1905 at famed 101 Ranch of Miller Brothers in Texas. Occasion was convention of National Editorial Writers. Few years earlier, militant Apache was labeled uncivilized savage. For a time a Geronimo car was made in Enid, Okla. (Bureau of Indian Affairs, National Archives) . . . Indians enjoyed posing in white man's thunder wagons (below) and auto merchants were happy to have shots for publicity purposes. (Div. of Manuscripts, University of Oklahoma).

ON A TRIBAL MISSION to Washington, D.C. these Indian leaders (right) posed in Pope-Toledo, circa 1905. Photo was taken by Carl H. Claudy, one of 5 organizers of National Highway Association in 1912. (The Smithsonian Institution).

FIVE CHIEFS in full feather war bonnets and native dress in Buick at Indian camp. (Div. of Manuscripts, University of Oklahoma Library).

DRIVER OF THIS WHITE STEAMER, like most pioneer motorists, was obviously proud of his vehicle. (Chas. Lytle Collection).

The END of the
BEGINNING

From the first Duryea to the Model A Ford, more than 1,500 makes of motor vehicles came and went. Hopeful manufacturers, from one end of the nation to the other, tried their luck on the giant roulette wheel of industry. They built the Hydromotor, the Ajax and the Eureka in Seattle, Washington; the Hanson and the Golden Eagle in Atlanta, Georgia; the Skene Steamer in Lewiston, Maine; and the Poppy Car, the Oldfield and the Kennedy (among others) in Los Angeles.

The variety was seemingly endless. The eight-wheeled Octoauto conceived by M. O. Reeves of Columbus, Indiana, was a theoretical success and a practical bust. The six-wheeled Pullman built in York, Pennsylvania, was little better. Three-wheelers—like the Kelsey Motorette, several models of the Knox Waterless, the Tinkham and the Trimo—had some acceptance before they disappeared.

One of the reasons there is so much confusion about the exact number of motor car makes is because of the many one-timers involved. Unknown mechanics in livery barns, woodsheds and corn crib alleys labored over personal masterpieces which they were convinced would make them rich and famous; some worked, some failed and others never got beyond the dream stage. Clifford Sklarek in Canton, Illinois; Vernon W. Miller in Brice, Ohio; Llewellyn Pickford in Palmerton, Pennsylvania; the Wreisner brothers in Dassel, Minnesota, and Robert Temple in Denver, Colorado, built cars which operated successfully but never made it to market. Even in Alaska in 1905 Robert E. Sheldon put together the territory's first workable gas-mobile from pictures and articles he had seen in newspapers and magazines.

It was the age of the assembled auto, a conglomerate mixture of parts available from a wide variety of suppliers, many of whom were also new at the game. These mongrel motor cars still stump the modern-day experts when they appear in old photographs. The Wahl Motor Sales Company of Detroit came up with a unique idea when it offered a ready-made auto on which dealers could display their own trademarks; had this concept caught on, researchers would never have been able to unravel the mess.

Still another interesting innovation was the do-it-yourself plan offered briefly by the C. H. Metz Company of Waltham, Massachusetts. In an effort to compete with the Model T in the low-price field, the firm developed a "knock-down" car which the buyer could assemble. The vehicle came in 14 separate packages,

each costing $27 which had to be paid before the next unit was shipped. The packages had to be taken in a prescribed order, with the vital elements contained in the final three boxes: Number 12 brought the engine; Number 13 the magneto; Number 14 the carburetor, fuel tank and crank. The Metz auto kit cost a total of $378, but even at that it did not quite capture the imagination of the American public.

Many of the automobiles which faded from the scene were not mechanical failures. Some were the victims of shaky finances, poor business management, feeble sales efforts or lack of advertising. The depressions of 1907 and 1929 took their toll; so did the economic curtailments of World War I and the deflationary period which followed. Others simply did not improve with the times, and when competitors updated, the laggards fell by the wayside.

There were occasional fads, of course, like the cyclecars—more than 120 different makes—which scooted about prior to World War I. For a time sporty runabouts like the Glide, the Covert, the Middleby, the Pickard and the Stutz Bearcat were the rage.

The three major power systems—steam, electric and gas—vied for acceptance in the early days. Each had its advantages and drawbacks, its supporters and detractors. The electrics were quiet, dependable, odorless and clean—but the limitations of the batteries and the problems of regeneration spelled their ultimate demise. The steamers were speedy, great at hill climbing and smooth operating—but they were slow to start and were forever running out of water. The gas cars—in spite of their racket, fumes and mechanical eccentricities—proved the most functional and adaptable to the demands of a fickle public. The farther out into the country the roads extended, the more the internal combustion engine overcame the attributes of the other two.

It was all part of a developmental evolution. What seemed so adequate in 1905 was obsolete a year later. Friction drive cars like the Metz, the Union and the Lambert made sense, but the technology of the period wasn't able to provide the materials to avoid disc slippage. The sudden undoing of more than 70 different makes of high-wheelers was another notable example.

In retrospect, the continuing changes—and the reasons for them—are generally quite obvious. To those who lived during the age of automotive adolescence, the pattern was far less distinct. It was a

learn-as-you-go process with no precedents to follow or pitfalls to anticipate. Among the manufacturers, for every fortune made, hundreds of air castles crumbled. Among the motorists themselves—the great **hoi polloi** of the highways—the concern was less for how the autos came about, but how to own one and keep it operating.

Pioneer drivers were seldom interested in the problems of Thomas B. Jeffery or Henry M. Leland. They did, however, fret about such picayunish but pesky details as the buttoning down of side-curtains in a sudden squall, the stoking of a Clark charcoal auto heater, the frustration of a broken drive-chain wrapped around a rear axle, the feeble flicker of a carbide lamp on a dark country road or the endless polishing of brass "brightwork."

From it all emerged the modern American automobile—the mechanical Jekyll and Hyde which was to bring so many mixed blessings to future generations. It took some 6,000 years to progress from the invention of the wheel to the unveiling of the first Duryea; two decades later the once-scorned horseless carriage was a permanent fixture. Charles J. Glidden, who had done so much to foster its acceptance, was to write in 1911: ". . . . our whole mode of life has been changed by the motor car . . . It has brought God's green fields and pure air nearer to our hives of industry."

ITS UNIQUE WOODEN AXLE characterized jaunty Brush Runabout (left). Here F. A. Trinkle and wife were about to leave Denver in 1908 for San Francisco, after he successfully completed motor trip to summit of Pikes Peak. (Denver Public Library Western Collection).

JONATHAN DIXON MAXWELL'S popular auto (top left) finally succumbed in mid-20s but its memory lingered on . . . Note unusual spring-suspension wheels on this vintage cab (top center) . . . An early Chevrolet wrecker (top right). (Photos left to right—The Kansas State Historical Society; The Smithsonian Institution; General Motors Corp.).

OLDSMOBILE JUGGERNAUT (below) was far cry from its rickety ancestor built in 1897 (right). (Oldsmobile Div. General Motors Corp.).

FIRST PRODUCTION four-wheel drive auto (above) built by FWD Corporation, rolled out of Clintonville, Wisc. shop in 1911—and was never sold. It was used as demonstrator, and when firm shifted entirely to motor truck manufacturing, it was used for nearly 35 years to haul company mail to and from post office. (FWD Corp.).

POPE-TOLEDO WAS ADVERTISED as "The Quiet Mile-a-Minute Car." It was made in Toledo, Ohio, which with advent of John North Willys, became for a time the nation's second city in automobile production. (John A. Conde Collection).

AMERICAN LOCOMOTIVE COMPANY of Providence, R.I. took fling at auto manufacturing with its lumbering Alco. Company stressed longevity based on indestructibility of its exclusive alloy steels. Same Alco won 1909 and 1910 Vanderbilt Cup competition. 1912 model is shown above. (John A. Conde Collection) . . . Below is 1904 Rambler Model L featuring surrey top without fringe and wicker picnic baskets on side. It was especially popular for Sunday outings. (American Motors Corporation).

POPE-HARTFORD AUTOS (top left) were made in Hartford, Conn. from turn of century to advent of World War I. Col. George Pope was one of numerous bicycle manufacturers to switch to motor cars. In 1904 his company was criticized by other builders for including lamps as standard equipment. The Elmore auto (top center) was produced in Clyde, Ohio, by Elmore Motor Car Company for more than decade before brought into General Motors combine. It was advertised as "The car that has no valves." (Photos John A. Conde Collection). Tiller-steered two-seater (top right) with lamp on front axle and gong on dash, was first auto in Benson, Minn. (Minnesota Historical Society).

COLE MOTOR CAR COMPANY of Indianapolis, Ind. (left) was in production from 1910 to 1925. During first three decades of auto manufacturing, morta'ity rate of such firms was extremely high, though reasons for failure varied considerably. (The Smithsonian Institution).

DORT AUTOMOBILE—1921 model shown below—was named for J. Dallas Dort, early partner of William C. Durant in carriage building business. Car persisted on market for about 10 years. (John A. Conde Collection).

WHILE OTHER AIR-COOLED AUTOS faded into automotive oblivion, popular Franklin (above left) stayed competitive for more than 3 decades. It was made by H. H. Franklin Manufacturing Company of Syracuse, N.Y. and in its lifetime underwent several major appearance changes, one of most distinctive being shovel-nose of this 1905 model. (John A. Conde Collection) . . . Rollin White, one of 3 sons of Cleveland, Ohio, sewing machine, roller skate and bicycle manufacturer, perfected flash boiler for steam automobiles in 1899. His concept gave early White Steamers an edge over most contemporaries. Model shown (above center) was driven by Chairman Augustus Post of 1905 Glidden Tour. (Pennsylvania Historical and Museum Commission).

PLINEY OLDS—father of Ransom E. Olds—posed (above) in one of his son's earliest Reos. After success of his curved-dash runabouts, the younger Olds sold his interest in Olds Motor Works and organized Reo Motor Car Company in 1904. (Pennsylvania Historical and Museum Commission).

THE LUVERNE (above right) was produced in its namesake town in Minnesota. Until great industrial shakedown following World War I autos were made in many unlikely cities, such as Angus, Nebr.; Gresham, Ore.; Emeryville, Calif.; Comanche, Texas; Hutchinson, Kansas. (Minnesota Historical Society).

AMONG HUNDREDS OF MAKES which came and went in formative years, was the Regal (right), produced in Detroit from 1908 until deflationary period after World War I which took heavy toll of companies. (Edwin J. Sunde Collection) . . . The short-lived Ruxton (below) was unusual front-wheel-drive luxury auto manufactured by New Era Motors of New York from 1929 to 1931. Though its star rose and fell quickly, it did mark the beginning of new automotive era. (John A. Conde Collection).

SLOGANS OF NOTE

Lancamobile	"Automobilism Effectually Realized"	Santos-Dumont	"This One Flies But Never Falters
Black Motor Buggy	"Get There!"	Roamer	"America's Smartest Car"
Ariel	"Look for the Oval Front"	Owen Magnetic	"Banishing the Commonplace"
Paige-Detroit	"Highest Grade Small Car in the World"	Pilot	"The Car Ahead"
Fuller	"Fuller Cars Do Things"	Metz	"No Clutch to Slip—No Gears to Strip"
Lexington	"Built to Stay Young"	Dragon	"The Motor That Motes"
Pungs-Finch	"Stands Alone in Its Class"	Waverley Electric	"No Dirt, No Odor, No Grease, No Bother"
Henry	"Built to Sell on Its Merits"		
Commonwealth	"The Car With the Foundation"	Gasmobile	"The Finest Gasoline Touring Carriage Built in America"
Severin	"Faithful to the End of the Road"	Pope-Toledo	"The Quiet Mile-a-Minute Car"
Firestone Columbus	"The Car Complete"	Oakland	"The Car with a Conscience"
Elmore	"The Car That Has No Valves"	Brush	"Everyman's Car"
Union	"In Union there is Strength"	Parry	"In the Long Run a Parry"
Walter	"The Car of a Hundred Reasons"	Marmon	"The Easiest Riding Car in the World"
Bates	"Buy a Bates and Keep Your Dates"	Lozier	"The Choice of Men Who Know"

SELECTED BIBLIOGRAPHY

American Motors Corporation. *Rambler Family Album.* Detroit: 1961.

Anderson, Rudolph E. *The Story of the American Automobile.* Washington, D. C.: Public Affairs Press, 1950.

Automobile Manufacturers Association. *A Chronicle of the Automotive Industry in America 1893 - 1949.* Detroit: 1949.

——————. *Automobiles of America,* Detroit: Wayne State University Press, 1962.

Bergere, Thea, *Automobiles of Yesteryear.* New York: Dodd, Mead & Company, 1962.

Clymer, Floyd. *Motor Scrapbooks.* Numbers 1 through 6. Los Angeles: 1944-50.

——————. *Those Wonderful Old Automobiles.* New York: Bonanza Books, Crown Publishers, Inc., 1953.

——————. *Treasury of Early American Automobiles.* New York: McGraw-Hill Book Company, Inc., 1950.

Donovan, Frank. *Wheels for a Nation.* New York: Thomas Y. Crowell Company, 1965.

Ford Motor Company. *Ford at Fifty, 1903-1953.* New York: Simon and Schuster, Inc., 1953.

Giddens, Paul H. *Standard Oil Company (Indiana), Oil Pioneer of the Middle West.* New York: Appleton-Century-Crofts, Inc., 1955.

Glasscock, C. B. *The Gasoline Age.* New York: The Bobbs-Merrill Co., 1937.

Homans, James E. *Self-Propelled Vehicles.* New York: Theo. Audel & Company, 1908.

Karolevitz, Robert F. *This Was Trucking.* Seattle: Superior Publishing Company, 1966.

Lewis, Eugene W. *Motor Memories.* Detroit: Alved, Publishers, 1947.

Lief, Alfred. *The Firestone Story.* New York: McGraw-Hill Book Company, Inc., 1951.

Musselman, M. M., *Get a Horse.* Philadelphia-New York: J. B. Lippincott Company, 1950.

Pound, Arthur. *The Turning Wheel.* New York: Doubleday, Doran & Company, 1934.

Purdy, Ken W., *The Kings of the Road.* New York: Little, Brown and Company, 1949.

Rae, John B. *American Automobile Manufacturers.* Philadelphia: Chilton Company, 1959.

Rolt, L. T. C. *Horseless Carriage.* London: Constable and Company, Ltd., 1950.

Sibley, Hi. *Merry Old Mobiles on Parade.* Garden City, N.Y.: Garden City Books, 1951.

Smith, Philip Hillyer. *Wheels Within Wheels.* New York: Funk & Wagnalls, 1968.

Standard Oil Company (New Jersey). *The Lamp, 75th Anniversary of Jersey Standard.* New York: 1957.

Troyer, Howard William. *The Four Wheel Drive Story.* New York, Toronto, London: McGraw-Hill Company, Inc., 1954.

Tyler, Poyntz, ed. *American Highways Today.* New York: The H. W. Wilson Company, 1957.

White Motor Corporation. *The Albatross, A Quarter Century of White Transportation.* Cleveland: 1925.

Young, Clarena H. and Quinn, William A. *Foundation For Living; The Story of Charles Stewart Mott and Flint.* New York: McGraw-Hill Book Company, Inc., 1963.

Index

General

Alaska-Yukon-Pacific Exposition, 9, 52.
American Automobile Association, 12, 52, 73, 74, 81, 122, 123, 131, 139.
American Expeditionary Force, 145, 148.
American Locomotive Co., 181.
American Road Builders Association, 82.
Association of Licensed Automobile Manufacturers, 23, 52.
Automobile Blue Book, 131, 132, 158, 164.
Automobile Club of America, 53.
Automobile Club of Minneapolis, 91.
Automobile Gasoline Co., 105, 109.
Automobile Magazine, 13, 42, 122, 157.

Babcock, H. H., Co., 53.
Badger Four Wheel Drive Auto Co., 29.
Baker Motor Vehicle Co., 16.
Barnum & Bailey Circus, 53.
Boston Herald, 158.
Brush Runabout Co., 144.
Buick Motor Car Co., 24, 50, 108.

Cadillac Automobile Co., 24, 31.
California State Automobile Association, 132, 133.
Chevrolet Motor Co., 32.
Chicago Times-Herald, 13, 26, 51.
Chicago Tribune, 42.
Chicago Post, 74, 76.
Cole Motor Car Co., 182.
Columbia Motor Co., 23.
Cosmopolitan Race, 51.

Day Automobile Co., 144.
Dayton Engineering Laboratories Co. (Delco), 24, 36, 84, 150, 159.
De la Vergne Refrigerating Machine Co., 51.
Devils Lake Daily Journal, 74.
Duerr, C. A. & Co., 23.
Duryea Motor Wagon Co., 12, 144.
Electric Vehicle Co., 23.
Elmore Motor Co., 182.
Eno Foundation, 122.
Ernest Holmes Co., 119.
Ethyl gasoline, 104.
Ethyl Gasoline Corp., 107.
Farmers' Anti-Automobile Society, 122.
Federal Aid Road Act of 1916, 83.
Fisher Body Co., 31.
Flint Automobile Co., 53.
Ford Motor Co., 24, 35, 123.
Ford Times, 144.
Four Wheel Drive Corp. (FWD), 25, 159, 180.

Franklin, H. H., Manufacturing Co., 184.
General Motors Co. (Corp.), 24, 34, 96, 107, 182.
Geronimo Motor Co., 168.
Glacier Park Blazer, 74, 76.
Glidden tours, 2, 29, 35, 73-75, 78, 79, 86, 117, 158, 184.
Goodrich, B. F., Co., 132, 140.
Goodyear Tire and Rubber Co., 150.
Great Northern Railway, 74, 75, 79.
Grigsby Manufacturing Co., 96.
Gulf Oil Co., 131.
Harrold's Motor Car Co., 66.
Haynes-Apperson Automobile Co., 158.
Hine-Watt Manufacturing Co., 96.
Horseless Age, 114.

Indianapolis 500, 38.
Indianapolis Speedway, 52, 57, 83.
Johnson Service Co., 146, 151.
Kahn-Wadsworth bill, 83.
Krit Motor Car Co., 74.
Lawson, F. H. Co., 96.
League of American Wheelmen, 81, 82.
Le Matin, 52.
Lewis and Clark Centennial Exposition, 65, 67, 71.
Life, 13, 129.
Lincoln Highway Association, 44.
Little Motor Co., 32.
Louisiana Purchase Exposition, 52, 73, 139.

Macy, R. H., & Co., 51.
Madison Square Garden, 53, 62.
Maxwell Motor Corp., 26, 158.
McClure's Magazine, 131.
Metz Auto Co., 74, 177.
Minneapolis Journal, 62.
Motocycle, The, 12.
Mueller, H., & Sons, 51.
Munsey's Magazine, 53.
Munzer, Rudolph W., & Sons, 74.
National Automobile Show, 53, 62.
National Good Roads Association, 65.
National Highway Association, 175.
National Safety Council, 123.
New Era Motors, 185.
New York Auto Show, 159.
New York Times, 13.
New York Tribune, 121.
Oakland Motor Car Co., 24.
Olds Motor Vehicle Co., 33.
Olds Motor Works, 24, 35, 53, 59, 65, 67, 184.
Oriental Oil Co., 105.
Packard Motor Car Co., 44.
Pan-Pacific Exposition, 44, 149.
Peerless Motor Co., 24.

Philadelphia-Lancaster Turnpike, 82.
Portland Automobile Club, 67.
Prest-O-Lite Co., 24, 83.

Red Flag Law, 12, 122.
Reo Motor Car Co., 184.
Republic Motor Co., 32.
Review of Reviews, 42.
Rural Free Delivery, 144.

Saxon Motor Car Corp., 159.
Scientific American, 42, 144.
Sears, Roebuck and Co., 24, 144.
Signal Corps, 154.
Smith, A. O., Corp., 24.
Smithsonian Institution, The, 14.
Standard Oil Company, 106.
Standard Oil Company of California, 105.
Standard Oil Company of New Jersey, 107.
Sterling Bicycle Co., 21.
Studebaker Corp., 168.

Tice Law, 83.
United States Motor Car Corp., 24.
U. S. Army, 28, 145, 154.
U. S. Bureau of Public Roads, 12, 83.
U. S. Office of Public Roads, 65.
U. S. Office of Road Inquiry, 12, 82.
U. S. Post Office Department, 144, 146.

Vanderbilt Cup Race, 52, 181.
Vaseline, 106.
Wahl Motor Sales Co., 177.
Waltham Manufacturing Co., 144, 146.
Welch Motor Car Co., 165.
Wells Fargo Co., 149.
Winton Motor Carriage Co., 17.
Woods Motor Vehicle Co., 154.
Wooster Pike, 82.

People

Abbott, James W., 65.
Adams, Harry, 122.
Allison, James A., 24.
Apperson brothers, 16.
Apperson, Edgar, 23.
Apperson, Elmer, 23, 158.
Atwood, Margaret, 158.
Baker, E. G., 167.
Balger, Stephen M., 16.
Barthel, Oliver E., 58.
Bates, Luella, 159.
Baxter, Sylvester, 42.
Benz, Carl, 12, 32.
Benz, Carla, 32.
Berkebile, Don H., 14.
Besserdich, William A., 25, 29.
Bird, Anthony, 23.
Birnie, Harold T., 122.

Black, Charles R., 23.
Blanchard, Thomas, 12.
Bollee-Pere, Amedee, 12.
Boyd, T. A., 106.
Brazier, H. Bartol, 24.
Briscoe, Benjamin, 24.
Bryan, William Jennings, 172.
Budd, Edward G., 24.
Buick, David D., 24, 30, 108.
Burke, Mrs. Alice S., 159.
Burton, Dr. William M., 106.

Callihan, E. S., 10.
Cantor, Eddie, 173.
Carter, Byron T., 159.
Cato, J. L., 24.
Chevrolet, Louis, 24, 32, 34, 167, 168.
Chrysler, Walter P., 24, 26.
Claudy, Carl H., 88, 175.
Cody, Buffalo Bill, 167, 172.
Coolidge, Pres. Calvin, 166.
Cooper, Gary, 170.
Cord, E. L., 24.
Crocker, Sewell K., 65.
Cugnot, Nicholas J., 11, 12.
Cuneo, Mrs. Newton J., 158.

Daimler, Gottlieb, 12, 32.
Dallery, Charles, 12.
Dodge, Horace, 24, 35, 54.
Dodge, John, 24, 35, 54.
Dort, J. Dallas, 183.
Drake, Edwin L., 105.
Dudgeon, Richard, 12, 122.
Duesenberg brothers, 24.
Duesenberg, August, 168.
Duesenberg, Fred, 168.
Dunlop, John B., 81.
Durant, Mr. and Mrs. Clifford, 32.
Durant, William C., 24, 30, 32, 34, 108, 168, 183.
Duryea brothers, 14, 16, 23, 81, 114, 143.
Duryea, Charles E., 12, 26, 107.
Duryea, J. Frank, 12, 26, 51.
Duryea, Rhea, 107.
Dutton, Dr. Charles E., 74.

Edison, Thomas A., 9, 24, 37, 100, 167, 170.
Eisenhower, Lt. Col. Dwight D., 28.
Eno, William P., 122, 129.
Evans, Oliver, 11, 81.
Everitt, Barney, 168.

Fanning, F. J., 24.
Fetch, Tom, 54, 65.
Firestone, Harvey S., Sr., 24, 28, 37, 97.
Fish, Mrs. Stuyvesant, 157.
Fisher brothers, 24, 31.
Fisher, Carl G., 24, 83.
Ford, Henry, 16, 19, 23, 24, 27, 37, 52, 58, 95-97, 100, 103, 107, 112, 131, 143, 144, 155, 168.
French, Anne, 157.
French, Dr. William B., 157.
Geronimo, 167, 174.

Geving, Martin, 113.
Glidden, Charles J., 29, 52, 73, 74, 139, 178.
Goode, H. W., 67, 71.
Goodrich, B. F., 17, 24.
Grant, Arthur W., 24.
Greenough, Louis, 122.
Grenner, Harry, 105.
Guggenheim, Robert, 52.
Gurney, Sir Goldsworthy, 12.

Hammond, Eugene T., 55, 65.
Hancock, Walter, 12.
Harrah, William F., 2.
Harrington, Bert S., Sr., 105.
Harrison, Pres. Benjamin, 82.
Haynes, Elwood G., 23, 127.
Hill, Louis W., Sr., 74, 75, 79.
Holden, C. Clarence, 24.
Hoover, Pres. Herbert, 123.
Hover, William A., 135.
Hudson, J. L., 61.
Hunt, George A., 127.
Huss, Dwight B., 66, 67, 71.

Jackson, Dr. H. Nelson, 65.
James, William H., 12.
Janes, William, 12.
Jay, Henry B., 44.
Jeffery, Charles T., 21.
Jeffery, Thomas B., 21, 24, 81, 178.
Johns, Hermine, 158.

Kasdorf, Paul, 136.
Kettering, Charles F., 24, 36, 106, 159.
Kiblinger, W. H., 24.
King, Charles B., 51.
Kinsey, Apollos, 12.
Klock, Percy L., 24.
Knight, Charles Y., 24.
Kohlsaat, H. H., 13, 51.

Laessig, Clem, 105.
Lambert, John W., 12, 20, 23.
Landon, Mrs. Mary, 158.
Langen, Eugene, 12.
Lauder, Sir Harry, 100, 173.
Lawson, H. J., 81.
Legg, Frederick C., 74.
Leland, Henry M., 178.
Lenoir, Etienne, 12.
Leon, Nell, 159, 164.
Lesley, J. P., 106.
Levassor, Emile, 51.
Lewis, Walter, 20.
Lindbergh, Charles A., 96.
Lindstrom, Jennie, 158.
Little, William, 32.

MacAdam, John L., 82.
Mack brothers, 24, 143.
Marcus, Siegfried, 12.
Marmon, Howard C., 24.
Marr, Walter L., 30.
Marriott, Fred, 52, 167.
Maxwell, Jonathan D., 15, 24, 179.
Maybach, Wilhelm, 12.
McClure, C. L., 6.
McKinley, Pres. William, 52, 167.

McLean, John, 105.
Megargel, Percy F., 66.
Metz, Charles, 35.
Moncrieff, J. A., 24.
Midgley, Thomas, Jr., 106.
Miller, Vernon W., 177.
Mix, Tom, 168, 170.
Mueller, Frederick, 51.
Mueller, Oscar, 51.
Munzer, Clarence, 75.
Murdock, William, 12.
Murphy, John D., 158.

Nash, Charles W., 24.

Oelrichs, Mrs. Herman, 157.
Oldfield, Barney, 38, 52, 58, 167, 170.
Olds, Pliney, 184.
Olds, Ransom E., 12, 15, 23, 24, 33, 42, 184.
Otto, Nikolaus A., 12.

Packard, James W., 24.
Pandolfo, Samuel C., 131.
Park, Dr. James D., 72, 75.
Patton, George S., Jr., 46.
Peddinghaus, L. L., 140.
Pershing, Gen. John J., 145, 148, 152, 168.
Phillips, Mrs. John H., 157.
Pickford, Llewellyn, 177.
Pierce, George N., 24.
Pierce, Percy, 73.
Piscorski, Dan J., 24.
Pomeroy, Greta, 157.
Pope, Albert A., 24, 81.
Pope, George, 182.
Post, Augustus, 29, 184.
Post, Daisy, 157.
Powell, Nettie, 158.

Ramsey, Mrs. John R., 158.
Read, Nathan, 12.
Reeves, M. O., 177.
Richardson, Nell, 159.
Rickenbacker, Capt. Eddie, 148, 168.
Riggs, Dr. T. F., 52.
Rockne, Knute, 168.
Roosevelt, Pres. Theodore, 173.
Roper, Silvester H., 12.

Schumann-Heink, Madame Ernestine, 170.
Scott, Bert W., 52.
Selden, George B., 12, 22-24.
Sheldon, Robert E., 177.
Sklarek, Clifford, 177.
Smith, Arthur O., 24, 27, 112.
Smith, C. J., 52.
Smith, Capt. Lowell, 170.
Smith, Sidney, 167.
Speer, Robert W., 155.
Stanchfield, Barton, 66.
Stanley brothers, 143.
Stanley, Freelan O., 24, 53.
Stanley, Francis E., 24.
Stone, Melville E., 67.
Studebaker, John M., 24.

Stutz, Harry C., 24.
Symington, William, 12.
Taft, Pres. William H., 52, 167, 169.
Temple, Robert, 177.
Thomas, Edwin R., 24.
Trevithick, Richard, 12.
Trinkle, Fred A., 59, 178.
Vanderbilt, Mrs. Frederick, 157.
Vanderbilt, William K., Jr., 52.
Vanderbilt, Mrs. William K., 157.
Villa, Pancho, 46, 145, 148.
Walker, John B., 53.
Westlake, Eddie, 74, 76.
White brothers, 24, 82, 143.
White, Rollin, 184.
White, William Allen, 42.
Whitman, L. L., 55, 65.
Whitney, William C., 23.
Wigle, Milford, 66, 67, 71.
Williams, Capt. Alexander A., 145.
Wills, C. Harold, 24.
Willys, John N., 24, 180.
Wilson, Pres. Woodrow, 83, 131,
    159, 167, 168.
Winton, Alexander, 17, 52, 58, 143,
    144.
Witt, Frank A., 75.
Woods, Charles E., 143.
Young, James, 105.
Zachow, Otto, 29.
Zeder, Fred, 26.

Places

Akron, Ohio, 37.
Alexandria, Minn., 74.
Amity, Ore., 24.
Angus, Neb., 185.
Arkansas City, Kans., 111.
Atherton, Calif., 92.
Atlanta, Ga., 145, 177.
Auburn, Ind., 24.
Baltimore, Md., 14.
Bar Harbor, Maine, 122.
Bellefontaine, Ohio, 82.
Benson, Minn., 182.
Blue Island, Ill., 136.
Boston, Mass., 82, 122.
Boulder, Colo., 18.
Bretton Woods, N. H., 73.
Brice, Ohio, 177.
Buffalo, N.Y., 52, 66, 132, 144.
Burlington, Vt., 65.
Canton, Ill., 177.
Cascade Mountains, 66, 71.
Chattanooga, Tenn., 119.
Chester, Va., 49.
Cheyenne, Wyo., 52.
Chicago, Ill., 12, 21, 24, 42, 51, 65,
    96, 122, 123, 127, 143, 154, 157.
Cincinnati, Ohio, 96.
Cleveland, Ohio, 16, 17, 52, 66, 82,
    123, 132, 144, 184.
Clintonville, Wisc., 29, 159, 180.
Clyde, Ohio, 182.

Columbus, Ind., 177.
Columbus, N. M., 145.
Columbus, Ohio, 109.
Comanche, Tex., 24, 185.
Crookston, Minn., 74.
Cynthiana, Ky., 42.
Dakota City., Neb., 132.
Dallas, Tex., 105.
Dassel, Minn., 177.
Davenport, Iowa, 66.
Dayton, Ohio, 104.
Decatur, Ill., 51.
Denver, Colo., 62, 108, 134, 135, 139.
    145, 149, 152, 155, 158, 161, 164.
    177, 178.
Detroit, Mich., 19, 24, 31, 50, 51, 61,
    73-75, 96, 123, 177, 185.
Devils Lake, N. D., 74, 76.
Dismal Swamp, Va., 16.
Dorrance, Kans., 113.
Emeryville, Calif., 185.
Emporia, Kans., 42.
Enid, Okla., 168, 174.
Erie, Pa., 66.
Estes Park, Colo., 6.
Fargo, N. D., 74, 75.
Fergus Falls, Minn., 74.
Fort Benjamin Harrison, Ind., 145.
Fort Snelling, Minn., 137.
Geneseo, Ill., 66.
Glacier Park, Mont., 72, 74.
Glasgow, Mont., 75.
Glencoe, Ill., 122.
Grand Canyon, 134.
Grand Forks, N. D., 74
Gresham, Ore., 185.
Grosse Point, Mich., 58.
Gwinner, N. D., 97, 114.
Hamtramck, Mich., 54.
Hartford, Conn., 82, 115.
Havre, Mont., 75.
Hosmer, Neb., 132.
Houston, Tex., 123.
Hutchinson, Kans., 185.
Indianapolis, Ind., 23, 132, 172, 182.
Iron Mountain, Mich., 37.
Ironton, Ohio, 84.
Irvington-on-the-Hudson, N. Y., 51.
Jacksonville, Fla., 73.
Kenosha, Wisc., 21.
Kokomo, Ind., 23.
Lansing, Mich., 50.
Laramie, Wyo., 68.
Lewiston, Maine, 177.
Little Rock, Ark., 42.
London, England, 99.
Long Island, N. Y., 52.
Los Angeles, Calif., 170, 177.
Louisville, Ky., 132.
Luverne, Minn., 185.
Manhattan, Kans., 165.
Marietta, Ohio, 140.
Maumee, Ohio, 42.

Memphis, Tenn., 105.
Milwaukee, Wisc., 24, 112, 146, 151.
Minneapolis, Minn., 58, 62, 74, 77,
    125, 138, 166.
Minot, N. D., 74.
Mitchell, S. D., 122.
Moundridge, Kans., 18.
Mount Desert, Maine, 122.
Mt. Hood, 66.
Mt. Rainier National Park, 140.
Mt. Washington, 53.
Narragansett Park, R. I., 51.
New Orleans, La., 74.
Newport, R. I., 52, 157, 159.
New York City., 12, 23, 24, 42, 51,
    52, 54, 55, 62, 65, 66, 73, 122, 129,
    139, 158, 185.
Norwalk, Ohio, 31.
Nunda, S. D., 113.
Ohio City, Ohio, 12, 20.
Omaha, Neb., 66, 68, 131, 132.
Oregon City, Ore., 67.
Ormond (Daytona) Beach, Fla., 52,
    59.
Osakis, Minn., 74.
Palmerton, Pa., 177.
Pauline, Ore., 71.
Pawtucket, R. I., 24.
Philadelphia, Pa., 11, 24, 30, 42, 51,
    82, 123.
Pierre, S. D., 52, 122.
Pikes Peak, 53, 59, 178.
Pittsburgh, Pa., 52.
Pocatello, Ida., 52.
Pontiac, Mich., 165.
Poplar, Mont., 75.
Porterville, Calif., 111.
Portland, Ore., 65-67, 71.
Pratt, Kans., 138.
Providence, R. I., 143, 181.
Ramona, Okla., 83.
Rochester, N. Y., 12, 52, 127.
Salt Lake City, Utah, 137.
San Francisco, Calif., 24, 54, 55,
    65, 118, 133, 149, 158, 178.
San Jose, Calif., 127.
Seattle, Wash., 9, 52, 105, 177.
Sioux City, Iowa, 131.
South Sioux City, Neb., 132.
Springfield, Ill., 169.
Springfield, Mass., 12, 114.
St. Cloud, Minn., 131.
St. Louis, Mo., 24, 52, 66, 73, 105,
    109, 139.
St. Paul, Minn., 74, 173.
Stoneham Mass., 52.
Stratford, N. J., 155.
Syracuse, N. Y., 66, 184.
Tacoma, Wash., 65.
Tipton, Ga., 73.
Titusville, Pa., 105.
Toledo, Ohio, 180.
Topeka, Kans., 165.
Tribune, Kans., 111.

Vienna, Austria, 12.
Volin, S. D., 136.

Waltham, Mass., 35, 74, 144, 146, 177.
Washington, D. C., 52, 117, 144, 145, 157, 162, 175.
Waukegan, Ill., 51.
Watertown, N. Y., 53.
Williston, N. D., 74.
Woonsocket, S. D., 10.

Yakima, Wash., 111.
York, Pa., 159, 177.
Yosemite National Park, 133.

Zook Spur, Iowa, 24.

Motor Vehicles

Abbott-Detroit, 159.
Acme, 52.
Ajax, 177.
Alco, 181.
Allis-Chalmers truck-tractor, 149.
Amplex, 159.
Ariel, 186.

Baker Electric, 16, 167-169.
Bates, 186.
Benz, 32, 51.
Black, 145, 186.
Bliss, 116.
Brown, 165.
Brush, 7, 13, 59, 178, 186.
Buick, 30, 50, 108, 159, 164, 175.

Cadillac, 53, 159, 170.
Cartercar, 9, 159.
Chalmers, 74.
Chandler, 153.
Chevrolet, 34, 155, 168, 179.
Chrysler, 26, 170.
Cole, 182.
Commonwealth, 186.
Covert, 177.

Day Utility Car, 144.
Detroit Electric, 27.
Dodge, 35, 46, 87.
Dort, 183.
Dragon, 186.
Duer, 145.
Duesenberg, 168.
Duryea Motor Wagon, 20, 26, 51, 53, 177, 178.

Elmore, 182, 186.
E-M-F, 86, 168.
Essex, 55, 137.
Eureka, 177.

Federal truck, 149.
Firestone Columbus, 186.
Ford, 19, 27, 52, 96, 144, 155, 177.
Ford, Model T, 12, 23, 24, 34, 40, 88, 94-97, 99-103, 107, 112, 114, 118, 132, 144, 147, 168.
Ford "999," 52, 58.

Ford Quadricycle, 12, 19, 143, 144.
Franklin, 88, 121, 144, 184.
Fuller, 186.
FWD, 180.

Gasmobile, 186.
Geronimo, 168, 174.
Glide, 177.
Golden Eagle, 177.
Great Smith, 165.

Hanson, 177.
Harris motor wagon, 14.
Haynes, 161.
Haynes-Apperson, 127.
Henry, 186.
Holsman, 145.
Hudson, 60, 61, 148, 173.
Hupmobile, 24, 52, 53, 74, 75.
Hydromotor, 177.

IHC Auto Buggy, 145.
IHC Auto Wagon, 47.
International Harvester truck, 149.
Italia, 52.

Jeffrey Quad truck, 148.
Jewel, 145.
Johnson truck, ambulance, 146, 151.

Kelly-Springfield truck, 118.
Kelsey Motorette, 177.
Kennedy, 177.
Kiblinger, 145, 151.
Kimball Electric, 162.
Kissel Kar, 52.
Knox Waterless, 177.
K.R.I.T., 75.

Lambert, 177.
Lancamobile, 186.
Leach, 170.
Lexington, 186.
Little, 74.
Locomobile, 16, 52, 74, 75, 144, 157, 167, 174.
Lozier, 186.
Luverne, 185.

Marmon, 74, 75, 186.
Marvel, 163.
Mason, 168.
Maxwell, 26, 39, 113, 158, 179.
McIntyre, 145.
Mercedes, 52.
Mercer, 159.
Metz, 35, 74, 75, 83, 177, 186.
Middleby, 177.
Mitchell, 74, 75, 77.
Mobile Steamer, 53.
Moline, 144.
Moon, 74.
Morris & Salom Electrobat, 51.
Motor Drag, 51.

Nash Quad truck, 154.
National, 172.

Oakland, 24, 186.

Octoauto, 177.
Oldfield, 170, 177.
Oldsmobile, 15, 33, 52, 55, 59, 60, 62, 65-67, 81, 179.
Orient Buckboard, 35, 144, 146.
Oruktor Amphibolos, 11, 81.
Owen Magnetic, 186.

Packard, 54, 65, 74, 130, 163, 168, 170.
Paige, 74, 162.
Paige-Detroit, 186.
Panhard-Levassor, 51, 52.
Parry, 159, 186.
Peugeot, 38.
Pickard, 177.
Pierce-Arrow, 66, 73, 167, 169.
Pilot, 186.
Pope-Hartford, 182.
Pope-Toledo, 53, 58, 175, 180, 186.
Poppy Car, 177.
Premier, 74, 93.
Protos, 52.
Pullman, 159, 177.
Pungs-French, 186.

Rainier, 7.
Rambler, 21, 127, 136, 140, 141, 144, 149, 151, 172, 181.
Regal, 185.
Reliable Dayton, 145.
Reo, 33, 39, 184.
Rickenbacker, 7, 168, 170.
Rikker Electric, 51.
Roamer, 186.
Rockne, 168.
Rogers, 51.
Ruxton, 185.

Santos-Dumont, 186.
Saxon, 159.
Schact, 145.
Sears Motor Buggy, 24, 53, 144.
Severin, 186.
Shawmut, 52.
Skelton, 161.
Skene Steamer, 177.
Springfield, 169.
Stanley Steamer, 6, 52, 53.
Stearns, 52.
Studebaker, 17, 30, 168, 170.
Sturgis Electric Motocycle, 51.
Stutz, 74, 75, 177.

Thomas Flyer, 52.
Tinkham, 177.
Toledo, 134.
Trimo, 177.

Union, 177, 186.

Walter, 186.
Waverly Electric, 186.
Welch, 165.
White Steamer, 9, 29, 68, 117, 163, 167, 169, 177, 184.
White truck, 150.
Winton, 62, 65, 74, 154.

THE END